G000096251

THE
WINE
MEN

THE
WINE
MEN

Fiona Beeston

SINCLAIR~STEVENSON LTD

First published in Great Britain by
Sinclair-Stevenson Limited
7/8 Kenrick Mews
London SW7 3HG, England

British Library Cataloguing in Publication Data
A CIP catalogue record for this book is available from the British Library.
ISBN: 1 85619 051 X

Typeset by Butler & Tanner Ltd
Printed and bound in Great Britain by
Butler & Tanner Ltd, Frome and London

TO
BARBARA BRAY

ILLUSTRATION
ACKNOWLEDGEMENTS

The illustrations between pages 82 and 83 are reproduced by kind permission of the following: *Louis Monier*: Lucien Legrand, *Val de Loire*: Charles Joguet, *Alain Gagnez*: Jean-Paul Gardère, *Jacques Guillard/ Scope*: Eloi Dürrbach, *Michel Guillard/Scope*: Georges Lepré, *Françoise Saur*: Léonard Humbrecht.

CONTENTS

Introduction
xi

Lucien Legrand
1

Charles Joguet
13

Pierre-Jacques Druet
25

Jules Mabileau
35

Nicolas Joly
45

Georges Lepré
57

Claude Ricard
67

CONTENTS

Jean-Paul Gardère
77

Jenny Bailey
89

Eloi Dürrbach
97

Jean-Baptiste Besse
105

Bruno Clair
115

Jacky Confuron
127

Léonard Humbrecht
135

Michel Bettane
145

Conclusion
155

Addresses
156

Glossary
169

Index
173

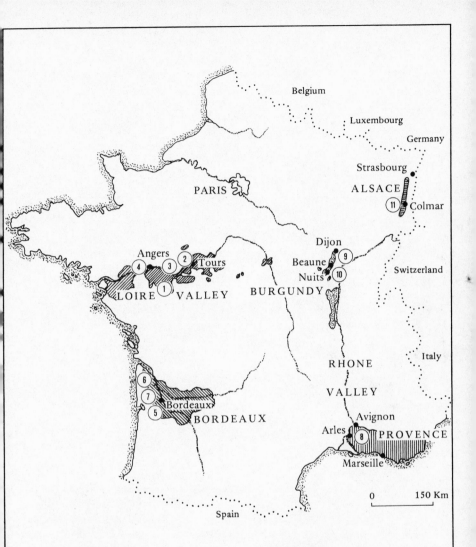

LOIRE VALLEY
(1) Charles JOGUET (Chinon)
(2) P.J.DRUET (Bourgueil)
(3) Jules MABILEAU
    (St-Nicolas-de-Bourgueil)
(4) Nicolas JOLY (Savennières)

BORDEAUX
(5) Claude RICARD (Graves)
(6) J.P.GARDÈRE (Pauillac)
(7) Jenny BAILEY (Haut Médoc)

PROVENCE
(8) Eloi DÜRRBACH
    (Coteaux d'Aix-en-Provence
    Les Baux-de-Provence)

BURGUNDY
(9) Bruno CLAIR (Marsannay)
(10) Jacky CONFURON-ĆOTETIDOT
    (Vosne-Romanée)

ALSACE
(11) Léonard HUMBRECHT
    (Alsace and Alsace Grands-Crus)

INTRODUCTION

EVERY YEAR in the Lycée in pre-war Beirut, Madame Debonne started the autumn term by reading us a description of the *vendange*, or grape harvest, in Burgundy.

It would be another decade before I took part in the ritual I heard about then, but the French obsession with wine and its mystique already seemed exotic and alluring even in that distant setting.

My curiosity was rearoused in my teens, thanks to the mediocrity of a lot of American wine in the 1970s. My father, a foreign correspondent, had by then been posted to Washington DC. This was just before wine became fashionable, when there were more connoisseurs of a dry martini than of a good bottle of Meursault.

When I was sixteen I criticised a cheap and, I thought, particularly nasty Californian wine that my father served at a dinner party.

'What do you know about it?' he asked testily.

I realised I knew absolutely nothing. But I decided there and then that I'd learn. A few years later, I felt I had tried everything: from washing glasses in a London wine bar to being a secretary for a wine importer. Wine still remained a mystery.

So I set off to work as an apprentice in the cellars of a small château in Bordeaux. I felt my career really began there – literally at the bottom – cleaning out the sludge from the grapes, wearing

long rubber boots and carrying a miner's lamp, clambering down
into the deep dark vats.

As a foreign woman working in one of the bastions of French
male society, I quickly became an object of curiosity. My work led
me all along the ancient route, through every stage of wine
producing, from picking and pressing the grapes in Bordeaux and
assisting the birth of a new wine, to the detached and clinical world
of blind tastings in London. During these group tastings – often
held at eight o'clock in the morning – I learnt to recognise wines
from different countries of the world.

My fourteen years in wine, in the vineyards and the cellars, as
a merchant and as a writer, have taught me one thing: quality
wines are not an abstract or a chance product; they are the creation
of man in harmony with the soil. My association with the men I
have encountered in the course of my training has had a profound
effect on me. It is they who have helped me to understand what
wine is really all about. Some of them produce aristocratic wines,
known throughout the world. Others have hardly strayed outside
their home villages.

Whether direct descendants of fifteenth-century wine producers,
ex-international bankers or advocates of organic farming, they
share one objective – to extract from the soil the best possible
wine, no matter what the cost in terms of money or effort.

The Wine Men is purely personal, and not at all intended as
a complete or balanced guide book. Important regions such as
Champagne and the Côtes-du-Rhône are not included. I am particularly attached to the Loire Valley and have given extra space
to the wines from this region. They have a wonderful and unique
capacity for mingling sensuality with elegance and deserve to be
better known.

The aim of this book is to help understand what wine is all
about. Over the last decade or so, wine enthusiasts, exasperated
with the mystification and snobbery that used to surround wine,
have taken off in an analytical and technical direction. It's true
they escaped from the old elitism, but new rituals were soon
established. A wine lover isn't admitted into the closed circle of

wine connoisseurs until he or she has learned all about the top winemakers' recipes: the fermentation temperatures, Brix content, origin of the oak casks, et cetera. Instead of drinking a glass of wine with pleasure, wine enthusiasts now try to outdo their colleagues with the latest inside information and trendy vocabulary. Yet identifying an aroma as nail-varnish remover or bananas doesn't necessarily increase the pleasure one gets from drinking it.

I firmly believe that getting to know the winemakers themselves is the key to understanding and appreciating their product. Wine is very much a reflection of the person who creates it. This book takes you through vineyards and cellars in the company of those who make the wines. You will meet, among others, the aristocratic owner of one of the finest Bordeaux vineyards, whose château could only be kept afloat by his becoming a door-to-door salesman; a young Burgundian who literally recreates vineyards by dynamiting land left fallow for over a century; a Loire producer who also collects menhirs (pre-historic monumental stones); as well as two great Paris wine merchants, a journalist who knows more about French wine than anyone else in the world, and the top wine waiter in Paris. They bring us a step closer to finding out what makes a wine tick, and above all to enjoying it.

Lucien Legrand

*O*F *ALL* my teachers in the wine world, Monsieur Legrand, one of the top Paris wine merchants, was my favourite. I spent five years selecting and selling wine with him, and listening to his Parisian-tinged philosophy. He took great pride in every task he did, no matter how small.

Every morning, for more than forty years, Lucien Legrand started his day with vigorous warming-up exercises. At eight o'clock on the dot, he would be on the pavement outside his shop, his greying 1950s moustache neatly trimmed, sporting his favourite blue check shirt and old leather jacket. With a broom in his hand, he would energetically sweep the front of his shop. It was his way of tuning in to the capital.

'I'm a Parisian through and through,' Lucien would say. 'There's nothing I can do about it. I was born here – Paris made me.'

M. Legrand's wine shop at No. 1 rue de la Banque still stands a few minutes' walk away from the Louvre, between the Palais Royal, the Place des Victoires and the Stock Exchange. Stockbrokers on their way to work would pause outside the shop and discuss their hunch on the day's trading ahead. His regular early morning customers would drop by and, amid peals of laughter, discuss their morning reflections with their favourite neighbourhood 'philosophe'. The shop's splendidly preserved 1900 decor made people feel time had stopped.

Before putting away his broom and dusters, M. Legrand would give a final glance over the shop-front to make sure that all the big glass jars of multi-coloured sweets were properly lined up under the red awning. This wide selection of old-fashioned sweets was one of M. Legrand's concessions to women and children.

'This shop was the first *épicerie fine*, or luxury grocery store, to open in Paris, at the turn of the century,' M. Legrand would tell any new customer, with pride. In the old days, great care was lavished on display. The shop still has its original 1900 wood panelling, cabled columns, mirrors and old oak drawers filled with strange delicacies and exotic spices. 'It was here that the first jar of imported English marmalade was sold,' he once told me, as if to underline the shop's adventurous beginnings.

The ceiling, entirely covered with corks, adds to the uniqueness of the shop's interior. But its main charm lies not in its decor, nor the wide and eclectic selection of wine, but in the human warmth it exudes.

Politicians and actors used to stop by to pick up a bottle of their favourite Bourgueil or Chambertin. But they also came to have a chat with their friend Lucien, to listen enchanted to this romantic Parisian's reaction to what made the city tick that week. But Lucien's friendliness was not reserved exclusively for the rich and famous. He had a wide range of friends who lived far removed from the spotlight, such as the much respected rubbish collector: every week for decades, he turned up at the shop with a load of empty bottles he had salvaged. In exchange, Lucien took him down to the cellar and let him choose a *bouteille de garde* (a *vin de garde* is a wine which requires bottle-age – around a minimum of ten years – to reach full maturity). The first time I met this somewhat odorous customer, Lucien told me he now had one of the best-stocked cellars in Paris.

I started to work in Lucien's wine annexe in one of the historic Paris arcades, the Galerie Vivienne, after a chance meeting with him in the gardens of the Palais Royal. As soon as he heard I was looking for a job in the wine trade, either in France or in California, he suggested I help him out in his old shop while waiting for something better to turn up.

I started by weighing out endless little bags of sweets and selling the odd bottle of wine. At the end of my first week, Lucien invited me to spend a weekend with the family in his house in the country. The weekend did not turn out to be the wine buff's paradise. We spent the entire time sanding down and waxing an old roll-top desk. However, I set to work with Lucien, and we chatted happily about this and that, matters of little importance. On Sunday evening before dinner, Lucien asked me, with a mocking look, if I liked the desk. Before I had a chance to answer, he said: 'It's yours. I've just bought a shop in the Galerie Vivienne that communicates with my old shop. I thought this desk might do there, and as you seem to have taken to it, the shop is yours.'

An unusual way of recruiting staff, but no doubt as effective as any other. In his new annexe, M. Legrand wanted to create a sort of small-scale cash-and-carry. He wasn't in the least interested in my wine background. He chose me to run it in the same way he selected his wines – by flair.

Lunch at the Legrand wine shop was always a special occasion for me. Every day at noon, the shutters went down on both shops, and all the employees went upstairs for lunch with the family. Any wine producers and *négociants* who happened to be in the shop would, of course, be invited up to share our meal. It was our way of keeping in touch with the latest news from the various vineyards.

In France at the beginning of the twentieth century a well-run family business could be identified by the quality of the food it served its staff. It was as if Lucien still believed in this, for he made sure that our lunches were not only excellent but copious. Lucie, his wife, who had retired to the country for a well-earned rest, spent most of her time in her garden, picking vegetables and fruit, pickling and preserving, and raising hens and rabbits to satisfy the healthy appetites of the Legrand household.

My first lunch above the shop got off to a bad start. Lucien Legrand, sitting as always at the head of the table, a woman on either side of him, poured me out a tumbler of Marcillac. This is a rustic, earthy wine from the Auvergne region, south of Clermont-Ferrand. It's a wine rarely seen on the export market, and I had never even heard of it. He asked me what I thought.

I was horrified. Usually I liked to taste before 11 a.m. when my taste buds were at their freshest, and I certainly would never agree to taste wine unless I used my own wine glasses.

I shot downstairs to get my special taster's glasses. But, meanwhile, the cook had done something unforgivable: she'd put a big casserole on the table and whisked off the lid. The whole room was filled with the stench of *tripes à la mode de Caen*. It was hopeless. I couldn't possibly taste in these conditions.

Lucien, who had watched my comings and goings in silence, burst out laughing. 'Mon Dieu!' he exclaimed, 'I can see I've got a huge task ahead of me, trying to educate an Anglo-Saxon!' He told me to stop fussing and drink my wine with my meal just like everyone else. Wine appreciation – the French method!

Lunch over the shop was always a lively affair. There was the Algerian delivery man; the Yugoslav cellarman, who at the slightest sign of a cold began his meal by eating an entire head of fresh garlic; the second delivery boy, a Cambodian; the Portuguese cook; the Breton accountant. Arguments always ended in laughter. Conversations covered the morning's usual range of problems, including the delivery boys' amorous adventures and, of course, stories about the customers. Lucien used to divide these into two groups: those who lived on the Left Bank – the *intellectuels* – and those who lived on the Right Bank – the *emmerdeurs* (trouble-makers). The well-off generally fell into the latter category and were almost always the most difficult to please.

Apart from the usual crowd at lunchtime, there were also regular weekly guests. These included the canon of the Cathedral of Notre Dame. He liked food and drink, and had never missed a single Friday lunch at Legrand's since the outbreak of the Second World War (when food was generally scarce).

But we did 'work' a little at lunchtime. It was then that we actually tasted the wines sold in the shop. This meant that all the employees, including the delivery boys, could advise customers on which wine was currently tasting its best. Needless to say, our daily seven-course lunches, though nourishing, were also somewhat exhausting for the less hardened! I was soon given my own bedroom, where a twenty-minute siesta restored my energy for the rest of the day.

For birthdays, Lucien would uncork his favourite *blanc de blancs*, the perfect aperitif wine. (*Blanc de blancs* is a champagne or sparkling wine made exclusively from white grapes. Traditionally, champagne is made from a blend of black and white grapes. The Pinot Noir grape gives the wine body, and the white Chardonnay grape gives delicacy and elegance.) Lucien was extremely proud of this champagne, which he sold under the Legrand label. It embodied an aspect of wine which he especially loved: just fresh and racy enough to whet the appetite, and bone dry.

To get the champagne as dry as he liked it, he had managed to persuade one of the producers to vinify a *cuvée* of wine *non-dosé* – long before it was fashionable to drink *extra brut* champagnes.

The *Legrand Filles et Fils* wine shop is considered to be among the best in Paris. It still has a range of *épicerie fine* products, though chiefly because they fit in so well with the turn-of-the-century decor. But before the War things were different.

'In those days,' he says, 'my parents ran the business, and they attracted their customers, as did most *épiceries fines*, first and foremost by the quality of their coffee, which was roasted at the back of the shop.'

Today the back-shop is lined with wine bins. But, in the old days, the stock reflected many more aspects of the way people lived. Methylated spirits were dispensed from a magnificent pear-shaped copper dispenser. Meths were used in every household for lighting and heating.

'In 1945 this building still didn't have any electricity or running hot water,' Lucien recalls. 'So keeping a house clean was no easy task. But it was something my mother prided herself on. Whenever a new shop assistant came to work for us, her first reflex was to sniff his feet! Her instinct proved right more often than not, and we'd see her rushing off to the chemist's to buy some formalin for the new employee to wash his feet in.'

The new arrivals were quick to learn that if they wanted to stay in Madame Legrand's good books, they had better not dirty their overalls too often. Dirty linen had to be taken all the way to the wash-boat moored off the Ile-Saint-Louis, a good three kilometres away.

'A quality *épicerie fine* always bottled its wines and spirits on the premises. Wine, port, rum, *crème de cassis*, cognac, calvados were all delivered in casks and barrels which had to be eased down to the cellar step by step. Each drink had its specific bottle shape and size, and the labels proudly declared: *Mise en bouteille par le maître épicier* (bottled by the master grocer).

'As a child, I saw the world through this shop and spent much of my free time with the shop assistants. I enjoyed being with them. They were simple souls, up from the country, whose only thoughts were what they would do on Saturday evening. They survived by instinct alone. We, on the other hand, were brought up in a rigid world whose only values were nationalism, and a shady form of patriotism verging on racism.

'The delivery boy's work particularly intrigued me. By far the most important qualification for the job was to be shrewd and a good negotiator. Only the very smartest of buildings had a goods lift, and deliveries by the main lift were, of course, forbidden. This meant that most goods had to be carried up by the service staircase. A real pro knew how to get access to the main lift, either by charming the concierge or, when that proved impossible, which was often the case, by craftily slipping past her lodge unnoticed.'

In 1945, Lucien took over the shop from his parents. In no time at all, his independent, slightly anarchistic outlook on life rubbed off on to its everyday running.

'The first thing I did was get rid of the starched white aprons – the grocer's uniform – we all wore. I had spent my entire life in uniform, from school to the army and again during my apprenticeship in the most highly regarded luxury grocery store in Paris, Félix Potin. It was time I had a bit of freedom of expression.'

M. Legrand, only interested in stocking quality products, soon set about changing his parents' successful range of branded wines. 'It was the in-thing to drink branded wines, but although I knew nothing about wine then, I did realise that selection didn't taste very good.' Rather than buy through a representative or a broker, as most grocers did at the time, he hit upon a novel idea: that of purchasing the wine direct from the producer. This was long before wine guides existed, and the only address of a wine producer he had was a vague acquaintance of his father-in-law's.

The winemaker in question lived in the Loire Valley, and Lucien set off to see him one Saturday evening in 1947, having picked up enough petrol coupons on the black market to get him there and back.

He returned with a barrel of dry white wine. It took all his talents of persuasion to push the new wine, for sweet wines were in fashion at the time. However, he soon built up a faithful clientele for it, and by 1949 he was travelling twice a month to Amboise to fill up his barrels. It was during that year that he became more adventurous and drove a further seventy kilometres, as far as the village of Chinon, to buy some of its red wine.

Later on, even after M. Legrand had built up a reputation as one of the best wine merchants in Paris and a talented discoverer of 'country' wines, he still went on selling his bottles in the same old way.

'Before I got to understand wine, I already knew how to sell it. There's no point in being a wine merchant if you don't know how to push the stuff. Having a fine, educated palate isn't enough to keep a shop going – you've also got to know how to work with your hands and your brains!

'The last thing a customer wants to hear is his merchant reciting a vineyard's technical statistics. What he wants is to be sure that each bottle he buys will give him immense pleasure.'

Lucien had a sixth sense when it came to understanding what customers wanted. One day a young woman entered the shop, looking for just a medium-priced bottle of wine. But Lucien sensed she wanted something special. With some encouragement, she revealed that the wine was to accompany a dinner she was preparing for a man she'd fallen in love with, though she hadn't dared tell him. Lucien disappeared down to the cellar and returned with a bottle of his own-label Burgundy, which we kept for our very best friends. Its haunting voluptuousness and lightness were just the right thing. Then he gave her some useful suggestions about the decor: the table, the candles, the food. Nothing too heavy. Keep everything fresh and light . . .

A few months later, the young customer returned and kissed M. Legrand on both cheeks. Their plot had worked.

In 1952, his love affair began with the fruity wines of Beaujolais. Without realising it, Lucien was about to become a trendsetter once again by selling a non-chaptalised Beaujolais Nouveau. (A non-chaptalised wine is one which has had no sugar added to it during fermentation. The widespread addition of sugar, or chaptalisation, in winemaking bumps up the wine's alcohol content. This gives it a sensation of roundness on the palate, but unless the sugar is added in very small quantities the wine becomes heavy and unbalanced, and usually leaves an unpleasant burning sensation on the palate.)

Lucien's fresh and innovative approach to buying wine soon began to attract notice.

'A well-known restaurant near the Stock Exchange, *Aux Lyon-nais*, heard that I travelled regularly to the vineyard to select my Beaujolais direct from the producer. It was so unusual for a grocer to take a real interest in wine that the restaurateur was intrigued and started to order his Beaujolais from me. Soon we were doing daily deliveries to his restaurant.'

But it was not really until the late 1950s that Lucien became fascinated by wine, and that his shelf space was increasingly taken up by bottles. At that time, he had still not been to Bordeaux, so one Sunday morning in 1961 he decided it was time he went. He put his bicycle and knapsack on a train and got off at the little town of Saint-André-de-Cubzac, east of Bordeaux.

'I knew no-one in the region and understood very little about what made wines from Bordeaux so special. I tasted wines at a few châteaux, crossed the Gironde by ferry, cycled through the Médoc, and at nightfall unrolled my sleeping bag in the nearby pine forests of the Landes. I enjoyed my solitary journey, but alas, the great revelation I was waiting for didn't come. I can't say I'm crazy about wines from Bordeaux – they've never been merry, festive wines.'

But today, Bordeaux is part of the Legrand family; one of Lucien's nine children started a small vineyard in the Entre-Deux-Mers region, which his widow now runs. But Lucien still has reservations about these 'dark, sly' wines.*

'I recognise the quality of the great Bordeaux,' he says, 'but they have too little sensuality for my taste. They're too strict, too severe, and far too intellectual to give any real pleasure.'

Nonetheless, M. Legrand did accept my very Anglo-Saxon pro-Bordeaux selection of wines in the Galerie Vivienne shop. I still feel there is nothing more aristocratic than a great Bordeaux. It must be something to do with their rectitude and unique elegance. In some strange way they fit – and, indeed, even reflect – a certain British attitude to life.

Lucien had a wonderful talent for unearthing 'country' wines at unbeatable prices. One day, France's most influential food and wine critics, Gault and Millau, published an article entitled *Legrand des petits crus* (Legrand, the king of little-known wines).

'That day I went up in the world. Gault and Millau had understood what really interested me. Anyone can buy a great wine – all you need is plenty of money. But try and find a wine that you'd enjoy drinking every day and you'll realise it's not so easy.'

Once, when we visited a wine producer in the Ardèche, M. Legrand got involved in a long discussion on the meaning of life and, before we knew it, it was lunchtime. The wine producer

---

* The Bordeaux wines haven't always enjoyed the reputation they have today. Saint-Simon, the famous seventeenth-century memoir writer, recounts how Louis XV once asked a minor dignitary from Bordeaux whether there were any drinkable Bordeaux wines. If you listened to the people of Bordeaux, the man told him, you'd think their wine was 'nectar fit for gods'. In his view, the wines had a 'dark, sly tang' but were not unpleasant, nevertheless.
Le Grand Dictionnaire de Cuisine, by Alexandre Dumas (Paris, 1873).

insisted that we share his frugal meal. He was setting off to his cellar to choose a bottle of fine wine when Lucien held him back. The wine he drank every day would suit us very well. The producer was slightly taken aback, but nonetheless poured us out his *vin ordinaire*. Lucien took a sip and his face lit up. This was the sort of wine he had been looking for. He bought all that the producer would let him have. The poor producer was astonished that anyone could be interested in a light, rustic wine made for home drinking.

It had just a fleeting taste of soft red fruit and, with a mere 9.5 per cent of alcohol, was wonderfully refreshing. Back in Paris, Lucien took out his pen, a piece of plain brown wrapping paper and, in his careful handwriting, wrote a straightforward label for his latest discovery. He named the wine '9.5' and sold it for 9.50F (£1). To this day, it's still one of my favourite summer picnic wines.

Lightness is almost a religion for Lucien Legrand. At the age of seventy-six, slim, bright and cheerful, he has remained faithful to the elegant image of the grocers of his youth.

'Grocers were always a proud lot, parading outside their shops in their starched white aprons. They were leaner and more sprightly than the butchers, they danced better than the other shopkeepers. And,' he adds with a touch of nostalgia, 'all the pretty girls fell for them!'

Lucien never wasted much time on heady, over-chaptalised wines. 'No-one eats the fat on meat any more. But people continue to drink hefty wine merely because they rarely have the choice of anything better. I realised many years ago that customers, given half a chance, prefer light, easy-to-digest wines. So I set off to see my favourite producer in the Beaujolais and got him to vinify a barrel of his *primeur* especially for me, without adding any sugar to it. He thought I was crazy and said I would never be able to sell such a light wine. He was right in that the wine had a low alcohol content, but it was deliciously fragrant and we'd sold out of it within a few days.'

Lucien used the names of neighbouring streets for his wines. It reinforced his feeling that he belonged to Paris. His most popular wine was called the Cuvée des Petits Pères named after the little square opposite the shop. (The square itself is named after a seventeenth-century Augustinian convent, abolished during the Revolution.) The labels were designed by Lucien and, of course, written in his own handwriting. Simple labels just like the wines he chose.

'The Cuvée des Petits Pères comes from the Côtes du Ventoux. It's an unfiltered, non-chaptalised, untamed, vibrant ripe wine full of pungent earthy aromas. A wine for those who really enjoy life. It's not for professional wine tasters – they wouldn't understand it!'

Lucien Legrand spent most of his life searching out unknown wines in often forgotten, remote vineyard areas. For him, wine is a reflection of its winemaker. He was always overjoyed when he discovered a 'new' producer with a strong personality. If it so happened that his wife looked young, healthy and delectable as well, so much the better. He could invariably say: 'Their wine has got to be as *épanoui*, or radiant, as they are.'

He attached great importance to his friendship with his various suppliers. Over a number of years, new discoveries became close friends. Wine was never an abstract product for Lucien, as it sometimes is with the new breed of wine buyers.

'Nowadays, professionals have samples mailed to them. They are tasted "blind" in tiled, clinical surroundings. Naturally, before any buying decision is taken, the wine is sent off to the lab to be analysed. And what's the outcome? Wines that all smell and taste the same: middle-of-the-road, compromise wines. Individual wines with powerful, original expressions are eliminated straightaway. The professional wine buyers may well wet their lips with wine, but try and find one who actually quaffs the stuff down. There aren't any! They've forgotten what pleasure is all about.

'Today's wine drinker, by showing too much awe and respect for this new generation of specialists, has entered on the slippery path towards squeaky-clean, chaptalised, over-oaked,* gutless

---

* Today's trend is to age red and white wines in new oak casks. This masks the wine's real vinous flavour and gives it a strong vanilla/oaky taste.

products, launched with a multi-million media bang.'

Lucien enjoys using colourful metaphors. Referring to today's oenologists who – according to him – no longer understand the simple pleasures of life, he says: 'They are gynaecologists who think they are Don Juans!'

At the age of seventy-five, Lucien Legrand handed over the running of his shop to Francine, one of his nine children, all of whom were born above the shop. But he keeps his nose in the wine business by occasionally going on buying trips with his son Yves, a wine wholesaler and retailer on the outskirts of Paris.

His retirement days in the country aren't as tranquil as he expected. Apart from the fact that he is a grandfather to twenty-four children, and about to become a great-grandfather, he's also an active town councillor, bubbling over with projects. All this just leaves him time to write a few poems in his enchanting old-fashioned handwriting. But, despite his numerous activities, Lucie, his wife, is glad to have her man back home. Even if she does still run the large vegetable garden single-handed.

Legrand Filles et Fils
1, rue de la Banque
75002 Paris
tel: 42.60.07.12

Le Chemin des Vignes
113 bis, avenue de Verdun
92130 Issy-les-Moulineaux
tel: 46.38.90.51

Charles Joguet

*C*HARLES JOGUET isn't very talkative. But his reserve is due not to any inflated self-importance but to his genuine modesty and sensitivity.

He doesn't like it when people, as they often do, draw on the superficial parallel between his work as a painter and sculptor and his life as a winemaker in Chinon. Yet journalists in the various media find it hard to resist this dual image which depicts the bearded artist, strolling through his vineyard in an open-necked shirt, as simultaneously a creator of artistic forms and a moulder of fine wines. That rather dilettante image doesn't give a true picture of Charles Joguet at all.

He already knew he wanted to become a painter when he was very young, and later on turned to sculpture. This was to be his life, his career, and not simply a hobby. In the 1950s, he went to art school in Paris – the then well-known Ateliers du Montparnasse – but, just as he was beginning to make a name for himself, his father died suddenly. As he couldn't leave his mother to run the family vineyard alone, Charles set about shouldering two careers at once. He planned to spend most of his time where he was happiest, painting in his Paris studio. But then the inevitable happened: he became increasingly fascinated by wine and started to spend more and more time in the vineyard. And eventually, his spectacular success at winemaking led him to spend more time in the country than in the city.

The arty wine producer doesn't exist. If you want to meet the sculptor, you'll have to try and track him down in his Paris studio. He goes there every weekend to be with his wife, a theatre critic, and, of course, to sculpt. His Paris life is full of exhibitions and visits to the theatres and cinema, and all the other experiences and encounters that may act as a source of inspiration for an artist's work.

It's probably much easier, however, to meet the wine producer. The quickest way is by uncorking a bottle of his Clos de la Dioterie, a wine produced from an 'historic' vineyard. (Charles' best growths enjoy the rare privilege in France of being sold under the name of *clos*, indicating that they come from a specific, distinguished vineyard, as with the great Burgundies.) Make sure you choose an older vintage. This wine, which is grown on a hillside, takes a good ten years to open out, and twenty to fifty before it is fully mature. The complex nose of liquorice and soft red fruit gives only a hint of the wine's unique and delicious taste: flavours of cloves, sloes and black olives mingle strangely yet exquisitely together. The wine is deep and very sophisticated, similar in many ways to a great Bordeaux, but less upright, less severe.

Needless to say, Charles Joguet refuses to be flattered by the praise his followers lavish on him, and sees things very much from his own point of view.

'In 1977 I went to Burgundy with my friend Jacques Puisais, the well-known Loire oenologist. I came back depressed and completely disoriented. We'd tasted some incredibly beautiful wines, absolute masterpieces. Back in my own cellar, I remember saying to myself: "You poor fool, what are you doing wasting so much time over a mere Chinon? No matter how hard you try, you're never going to get anywhere near the quality of the great Burgundies".'

Today, Charles Joguet is considered by many to be the creator of a new way of thinking about wine in the Loire Valley. He came late into the wine world and looked at winemaking from a new angle: an intellectual's viewpoint, stimulated and encouraged by Jacques Puisais. He questioned everything, promoted very old vines to star status, and invented a machine for crushing and treading grapes, the *machine à piger* – of which, more later.

In the early 1960s, however, nobody in the wine business had ever heard of Charles Joguet. Within his native village of Chinon, needless to say, there was a fair amount of talk about him; but he was far from being the great winemaker he is today.

One spring afternoon in 1964, Monsieur Taffonneau – a respected figure among Chinon wine producers – decided to pay Charles a visit. Old Taffonneau had heard rumours about this young eccentric who spent his time in Paris dabbling with paint while his poor mother worked on the property.

Partly out of politeness, but also out of curiosity, the old man asked Charles if he might taste his 1963 vintage. Charles poured him out a glass and nervously awaited the venerable expert's comments. In fairness it must be said that Joguet had started making wine at the beginning of a series of disastrous vintages which afflicted Touraine in 1960, 1963 and 1965. Old Taffonneau couldn't help pulling a face as he swallowed the wine his host had offered him: it was pale and sour – clearly this lad had absolutely no idea what winemaking was all about. He decided there and then to take him under his wing and show him some of the tricks of the trade.

'Taffonneau taught me everything there is to know about winemaking,' Charles maintains. 'For instance, I had no idea what chaptalisation was until he showed me how to add carefully measured amounts of sugar to fermenting grape juice.'

Charles Joguet followed Taffonneau's lessons with care. Over the years, the domaine's pale thin wines have become almost black in colour, deep and concentrated. Once Charles had got the feel for winemaking, he started to fine-tune on various aspects, such as getting his wines to express as fully as possible the *terroirs*, or soils, from which they came. Take the two-and-a-half hectare Clos de la Dioterie, for example – a vineyard already famous in the Middle Ages for producing quality wines. It is north-facing, which is unusual for a vineyard in the higher latitudes. Such sites are generally sought in warmer climates to reduce the vine's exposure to the burning sun. Yet, in the case of the Clos de la Dioterie, the sharp, almost pointed, acidity resulting from the northern exposure, associated with very rich tannins, works singularly well, producing a wonderfully lively and unexpectedly luscious wine.

But there is another secret that explains why this wine's real nobility only starts to express itself after forty to fifty years of bottle-age. This secret resides in the age of the vines themselves. At the Clos de la Dioterie, they are over seventy years old. At its peak, the wine releases a rich, earthy aroma which combines the smell of truffles and mossy undergrowth with animal scents such as 'the entrails of young hares' (as Jacques Puisais, with his precise yet original vocabulary, would say).

In the early days, practical considerations rather than any great feel for wine led to what turned out to be a major innovation.

'Like most farmers in the region, my father lived off a few hectares of mixed crops, including, of course, some vines. When he died in 1957, I realised that my mother couldn't possibly manage on her own, tending the vines and dealing with the sales as well. So I decided to spend a few days a month generally overseeing things and racking the odd barrel of wine from time to time.' ('Racking' is the siphoning-off of wine from its lees, or deposits, by pumping the clear wine into a clean cask or vat.)

'My mother used to sell our wine in bulk – as did everyone else in the area. To make things easier for her, I decided to bottle it, to save her the bother of having to draw wine from the vat every time a customer came by.' And so it was that the revolutionary commercial concept of domaine bottling in Touraine was sparked off in the early 1960s by a young man's desire to ease his mother's workload.

'The wine producers in the area thought of me as a sort of harmless fool! I was accepted by the community simply because I was the son of a wine producer. My eccentricities were tolerated, but it was painfully obvious that no-one took them, or me seriously!'

Charles soon realised that his fleeting visits weren't going to be enough to run the farm property adequately, so he began to spend a good deal more time there. One time-consuming job was the partial replanting of his Les Varennes vineyard. Les Varennes, with its chalky subsoil, produces fruity, light wines. Half of the vineyard had vigorous forty-year-old vines with the best of their life still ahead of them. However, the other half had one-hundred-year-old vines which had completely given up producing grapes.

A few years after the new vines were planted and started to produce, Charles Joguet couldn't bring himself to blend the wine from his young vines with the wine from the older ones. Without realising it, he was about to shake up his region once more with a second revolutionary idea.

'It may be delightful to see a grandmother with her grand-children. But when it comes to wine, I was horrified at the idea of imprisoning together in one bottle the vigour of a young vine and the wisdom and complexity of an older one. I simply couldn't bring myself to do it.'

Old vines have a well-developed root system. They dive deep down into the subsoil, where they reach rare minerals and trace elements. These are then taken up into the plant, and eventually leave their mark on the juice of the grape. Old vines are, of course, tired, and so less productive than younger ones. As they produce less, their sap feeds a smaller number of bunches. This gives a dense, complex wine, rich in fabric and with a touch of mystery – a wine requiring bottle-age.

Young vines, on the other hand, have a well-developed surface root system spreading out in the soil's upper layers, where the earth is generally more fertile. Needless to say, they produce prolific crops of grapes, making light, easy-to-drink, straightforward wines that give instant pleasure.

Charles Joguet couldn't bring himself to blend together and bottle such differing styles of wine even if they did come from a single vineyard. He eventually decided to vinify the juice from the old and young vines separately, and had two different sets of labels printed: one with the words *jeunes vignes*, or young vines, and the other *vieilles vignes*, or old vines. No-one had thought of doing that before.

This distinction has now become very trendy among wine drinkers, and is a very successful sales ploy. Producers across France boldly print *vieilles vignes* on their labels, and happily charge twice as much for their 'more concentrated, complex wine'. The problem is that, to date, no legislation exists covering the use of this wording on labels. A number of producers less scrupulous than Joguet happily hand out an old-age pensioner's certificate to vines which in reality are adolescents – a mere ten to fifteen years old.

With his inquisitive, open mind, Charles was bound to have the same sort of interests and concerns as Jacques Puisais. Soon after they met, he took one of Puisais' oenology courses, and they became great friends. Wine was by now one of Charles' great passions. But his vineyard was only large enough to keep him occupied part-time, and he still spent half the week in Paris. A casual conversation with an old school-friend from the village soon changed all that.

'We were chatting away about this and that when he asked me how much I thought the Chêne Vert vineyard in Chinon would fetch at the local auction. Of course, I'd known the vineyard with its centuries-old oak tree since I was a child, but I'd no idea it was up for sale. Although there was no question of my buying it – I simply hadn't the money – I decided to go along to the sale out of curiosity.'

It was an exaggeration to refer to the Chêne Vert, or Green Oak, as a vineyard. It had been a vineyard once, but the vines had been left to sprawl untended, and the steep slope was overrun with brambles and wild fennel. According to legend, some monks planted an oak tree in the eleventh century in much the same spot as the present one, which is thought to be descended from the original. These monks from the prosperous Abbaye de Bourgueil nearby are credited with being the first to introduce the Cabernet Franc variety to the Loire. Originally from Bordeaux, the Cabernet Franc is today the most widely planted red grape in the Loire. It has certain similarities to its 'cousin', the Cabernet Sauvignon, but gives less tannic wines. It is known for the elegant yet aromatic wines it produces.

The auction was to take place *à la bougie*, or by candlelight. This traditional rural method is still widely practised at auctions in the French countryside. At the start of the bidding, three small, very thin, fast-burning candles are lit. The successful bidder is the one who shouts his offer just as the last candle burns out.

Joguet had already made a few discreet inquiries in town. There were rumours that somebody was going to bid on behalf of a rich financier but, apart from that, there seemed to be little interest in buying the abandoned vineyard. On the day of the auction, the room was only half full. An old man with a weather-beaten face told a cluster of people that he wanted to buy the Chêne Vert so as to have more grazing for his sheep. Charles glanced around him. There wasn't a single wine producer in the room. His natural discretion proved useful: leaning alone against a wall, he was soon forgotten. The bidding started at a ridiculously low figure. Just when the flame of the third candle wavered, Charles shouted out – much to his own, and everyone else's surprise. Before anyone had a chance to react, the flame had gone out. The two hectares of the historic vineyard were his for next to nothing.

Set on one of the highest hills of Chinon, the vineyard faces south-south-west. This means that the vines are beautifully exposed to the sun and yet, by an ingenious calculation, the huge ancient oak tree never casts its shadow on the vines planted around it. But the Chêne Vert's real originality lies in the fact that it is made up of two very different types of soils. The vineyard is split straight down the middle: half of it has a dark heavy soil with largish stones, producing a structured powerful wine rather 'closed in' on itself. The other half is covered with a crumbly, flaky soil that gives a light, aromatic, expressive wine. The Cabernet Franc grapes from both soils blend together to produce a perfectly balanced wine. In Bordeaux, in order to produce a balanced wine, it is usually necessary to have a minimum of three different vine varieties: one to give tannin, the other softness and the third fruitiness. At the Chêne Vert, it is the two different types of soils that do the work, expressing themselves in differing ways through the same vine variety.

Luckily, Charles Joguet is a very patient man. He was going to have to wait an excruciatingly long time before he could see for himself just what an exceptional vineyard he had bought. The Chêne Vert was left fallow a further fifteen years – the time it took Charles to get enough money together to carry out a complete overhaul of the vineyard.

'The Chêne Vert is a good twelve kilometres from our house. When I bought it we were still using horses to get to the vineyards and plough them. Apart from anything else, the journey to and from the Chêne Vert would have taken up too much time. Life became easier and distance shorter when, in 1966, I bought my first tractor.'

The long-awaited restructuring of the vineyard began in 1975. Although today the vines are still very young, the wine shows great ageing potential. According to Charles Joguet, his 1985 shouldn't be drunk before 1997 at the earliest.

'As for the 1986, it should really be kept forty to fifty years in a good cellar. But', he adds, knowing all too well that most people don't have a wine producer's patience, 'the inquisitive drinkers who "sacrifice" a bottle now should be able to detect aromas of sloes, plums, oranges, liquorice, and even a touch of fennel.' Perhaps a whiff of the wild fennel that still grows in the thin soil under the ancient oak.

'Having spent my youth away from the farm, I suppose I may have looked at things from an unconventional angle when I finally did start to make wine,' Charles replies with modesty when asked about his third revolution: the *machine à piger*.

If, in the making of red wines, not enough tannin and colour is extracted from the grape skins and stalks, the grape juice will remain pale and relatively tasteless, and can never be transformed into a rich and complex wine. What was needed, Charles decided, was a machine that would crush and tread red grapes enabling the juice to remain in contact with the grape skins and stalks so as to extract colour and tannin from them.

Of course, in the old days, farmers used to think nothing of climbing into the vats of fermenting grape juice and treading the grapes themselves so as to get as much as they could out of the grape skins.

'To get a good extraction, each vat should really be trodden three times a day for at least an hour each time. It's physically exhausting work, and so – even with the best will in the world – it's generally badly done,' Charles explains.

One day, Charles Joguet and Jacques Puisais decided to attack the problem. There had to be a solution, a machine that could replace this frightful work. After endless discussions, and waste-paper baskets full of outlandish sketches, the two men finally came up with a drawing that looked plausible.

They rushed off to see a builder of local winery equipment, and showed him the sketch of their infernal machine. The lid of the vat was divided into four mobile sections – rather like the choppers of a helicopter – each blade able to stomp slowly up and down separately to the bottom of the vat, pushing down the 'cap'. (This is a thick, hard, compact layer formed by the solid parts of the grapes fermenting in a vat. During fermentation the force of the carbon dioxide generated in a vat is such that the 'cap' floats on the surface. It is very difficult to break up, but in order to extract the necessary colour, the 'cap' has to be immersed regularly and mixed with the fermenting grape juice.)

The bewildered constructor eventually agreed to work on the prototype. The final version looked not unlike a giant coffee per-colator. But, instead of a human hand, plunger, filter and ground coffee, there was a room full of levers, hydraulic jacks, gears, chains and motors!

Today, more sophisticated versions of the prototype are now used by a number of producers in the Loire Valley and elsewhere. They could almost be described as tannin – and colour – extracting machines, and they have replaced the old method of treading, which was not only physically tiring but often dangerous, too, because of the high levels of carbon dioxide given off by the fermenting grape juice.

It was time now for Charles to turn his mind back to his vineyards. His most recent experiment started with lengthy negotiations with the National Institute of Agricultural Research (INRA). Charles was haggling to obtain a permit. Ever since the nineteenth-century destruction of European vineyards by an insect called the phylloxera, it has been against the law in France to plant vines that are not grafted on to American root stocks. For some reason, the insect isn't attracted by these American roots, and so the plant survives.

Charles Joguet found it difficult to accept the fact that he would never be able to make wine from ungrafted French vines – wine that would taste as it had done in past centuries. He longed to be able to plant one hundred per cent French vines, even though he knew that their expected life-span would be very limited: the phylloxera insect is still alive and well – no one has yet come up with a means of eliminating it – and so, with time, it will chew its way through the succulent French roots and eventually kill the vine.

But in 1983, he finally got permission from INRA to go ahead and plant an experimental vineyard with ungrafted French vines. He was overjoyed. At last he would be able to taste wine that would express fully and purely his *terroir*. To date, Charles has harvested four crops from these vines. Every year the wine is carefully put aside, and Charles follows its evolution with pride.

'The difference between these and my grafted vines is very striking. The grapes and bunches are much smaller, producing a low yield. The wine is incredibly dark in colour, with a wonderful luminous quality that I haven't seen anywhere else. It also has a lower alcohol content than my other wines but, strangely enough, it tastes as full as if it were richer in alcohol. But most extraordinary of all, is the extreme subtlety and elegance of the taste. And the flavour just lingers on and on.' But then Charles curbs his enthusiasm and adds a warning note: 'Of course, it's still far too soon to come to any firm conclusions. Let's hope the vines hold out a few more years against the phylloxera, so that the experiment can continue a little longer.'

To get just a little closer to the mystery and spirit of the ancient ungrafted product, Charles Joguet would gladly sacrifice a few more rows of his grafted vines.

Charles Joguet
Clos de la Dioterie
Sazilly
37220 L'Ile Bouchard
tel: 47.58.55.53

UK IMPORTERS/DISTRIBUTORS

Adnams Wine Merchants
The Crown
High Street
Southwold
Suffolk 1P18 6DP
tel: 0502 724222

Berry Brothers & Rudd Ltd
3 St James's Street
London SW1A 1EG
tel: 071 839 9033

Haines Hanson & Clarke
17 Lettice Street
London SW6 4EH
tel: 071 736 7878

Justerini & Brooks Ltd
61 St James's Street
London SW1
tel: 071 493 8721

O W Loeb & Co Ltd
64 Southwark Bridge Road
London SE1 OAS
tel: 071 928 7750

Pierre-Jacques Druet

*P*IERRE-JACQUES DRUET'S father was a wine broker based near the town of Tours in the Loire Valley. His was a speculator's job where vast quantities of wine from all over France were bought and sold on price and alcohol content alone. These table wines of no pedigree were purchased without being tasted and were then blended with wines of similar calibre before being sold – often as cheap branded wines.

'You can see how my palate was formed!' Pierre-Jacques Druet jokes, his cheerful face breaking into a broad smile. Although he is forty-one, he has an innocent, altar-boy look about him which makes it difficult to guess his age. Nor does it give an inkling of the obstacles he had to overcome to establish himself as a wine grower. His youthful looks are no doubt largely due to his energetic and enthusiastic outlook.

He wasn't born the son of a château-owner, nor was he likely to inherit enough money to buy a vineyard. He just knew from the start that wine-making was his vocation. When he studied at a viticultural college in Burgundy, he was the only boy whose father did not run a vineyard. The school uniform consisted of a bicycle, oilskins and a pair of gumboots! One morning, when he and his classmates were rigged up in their gear and learning to prune vines, he made a solemn vow that one day, come what may, he would be a wine grower. Pierre-Jacques is exceedingly patient, but he also has a very stubborn and determined side to his character.

He completed his training in a highly efficient winery in Switzerland, and finished his studies with a flourish at the universities of Montpellier and Bordeaux, with a top grade in oenology. He then became a technical salesman, and introduced into France the revolutionary Bucher winepress, made in Switzerland. Unheard of at the time, this splendid piece of machinery is now considered the ultimate luxury in a modern winery, costing some 250,000F (£25,000). It caresses rather than crushes the grapes, and thereby avoids extracting the 'off-tastes' that often result from an over-zealous pressing of the grape stalks and skins.

A well-paid executive job was not, however, going to stand in the way of Pierre-Jacques' ultimate goal. A few years later, having managed to put aside some savings, he set out in search of a vineyard of his own.

'Vineyards don't just turn up. You've got to be prepared to spend a lot of time searching for one you like. But above all you've got to be very patient and not get discouraged. I had no set ideas about where I wanted to settle, but I did have two prerequisites: the vineyard had to be reasonably priced, and it had to be potentially capable of producing top-quality red wines.'

Producing white wine was out of the question. Pierre-Jacques knew only too well the French wine drinker's reluctance when it comes to white wines. And he certainly didn't want to be landed with stocks of bottles he couldn't sell on the home market, as well as all the other problems he'd have to face in getting his vineyard going.

The average French wine drinker has a strange attitude. Although he treats red wine with the utmost respect and often credits it with medicinal qualities, he regards white wine as the cause of all kinds of aches and pains. He seems to believe that if it doesn't make you nervy and jumpy, it will give you a headache; in either case, it will keep you awake at night. Doctors and oenologists have found no basis for these deeply felt convictions, and although there isn't the slightest trace of caffeine or other stimulants in white wine, the French continue to shy away from it and stick resolutely to red. Too bad. They'll never know what a great maker of white wines Pierre-Jacques could have been!

Pierre-Jacques, his wife Martine and his two children spent a trial period running a vineyard in the south of France. But, because of their gentle Loire accent, the locals treated them as foreigners and excluded them from village life. This wouldn't do for a family that very much wanted to be involved in their local community.

Nor did Pierre-Jacques waste any time in Burgundy. A 'foreigner' hasn't been able to buy land there since the fifteenth century! The sale of even a couple of rows of vines awakens the avarice of the entire province, and the land is eventually sold at ridiculously inflated prices.

Pierre-Jacques was, however, quite prepared to move to Bordeaux. He looked at a charming property in Saint-Emilion but finally backed away, uneasy at the thought of having to take out quite such a large bank loan.

He eventually found just what he was looking for outside Bourgueil, in the little village of Benais. Here his accent wasn't out of place and he is now considered one of the locals. The village is so much part of his life that he couldn't even contemplate moving to Saumur, although it is only a dozen kilometres away as the crow flies. He gets on well with his colleagues in Saumur-Champigny, and yet they seem to belong to a completely different viticultural world. It just goes to show that geographical borders in the wine world can only really be understood on foot or by bicycle.

'I was desperate. I'd searched for a property just about all over France but for some reason, not in my homeland, the Loire Valley. One day, as I was walking uphill through some vineyards near Bourgueil, I stumbled across some very old vines planted on a slope overlooking the village. Just looking at these dry, twisted plants – knotted like an old man's hand – I knew they must be at least fifty years old. So I went straight down to the village, and eventually discovered that they belonged to a widow. It turned out she'd been trying for some time to let her vineyard and her old somewhat run-down winery. I was overjoyed, and signed the lease straightaway. It was only afterwards that I felt a twinge of anxiety. My long-awaited adventure was about to begin, bringing with it its share of problems! However, at least I wasn't having to spend a huge sum of money on buying land, nor was I going to have to wait years for new vines to grow. I knew the old vines would produce a top-quality wine as from the very next harvest.

'Later on, I learned that Jacques Puisais, the respected Loire oenologist, had kept a log-book on those very vines for over two decades. Back in the 1960s, he had noticed that the hillside called Grand Mont, where "my" vines were planted, produced exceptional wines for long-keeping. Out of interest, he'd noted down at regular intervals information on such factors as the size of the crop, how the vines reacted to different weather conditions, etcetera. This 'bible' is still invaluable to me. It meant I was taking over vines I felt I knew. It also enabled me to take risks that I would never have dared to take otherwise.

'After the heavy rains of 1987, for example, I resisted the general panic in our region and decided to wait a little longer before harvesting. According to Puisais' observations on similar wet autumns, if the rain didn't go on for too long the grapes should be tough enough to resist the spread of rot. Instead of harvesting insipid grapes, swollen with rainwater, I just prayed that the sunny weather would return. It was a nerve-wracking wait. Eventually, I was the last person in the village to harvest, but I did pick under sunny skies, and I produced a concentrated wine that will easily keep another thirty to forty years. Not bad for a vintage that was generally considered to be a disaster!'

Pierre-Jacques was just over thirty years old when in June 1980, he arrived at the village of Bourgueil with his wife Martine, their two children and another on the way. The few houses to let in their area had been snapped up by the engineers working at the nearby nuclear power station. After weeks of house-hunting, they finally gave up and moved into the only place available: a council flat.

The council flat address that appeared on their first 'gold medal' wine put off many a potential buyer. Martine remembers only too well the disconcerted faces of the few customers who tracked them down and were prepared to climb the two flights of cabbage-green stairs to their front door.

Every profession has to live up to some kind of folksy image. And the traditional picture of a winemaker with a bulbous red nose appearing from behind a cask with a dusty old bottle in his hand did not square with the council-flat aura. So, whenever a new customer rang the door bell, Martine would quickly drop whatever she was doing, scooping up a child as she went, and whisk the bewildered caller off to the winery her husband shared with the old widow. Here, the sight of casks and cobwebs and the smell of wine helped create the right sort of atmosphere and reassured startled customers.

Overall, Pierre-Jacques doesn't have particularly fond memories of his first years in Bourgueil. The people of Touraine are extremely convivial and generous – once they get to know you. But that doesn't happen overnight. And before they extend their hospitality there can be a period when they are, to put it bluntly, sly and suspicious. The villagers were there watching and waiting for the oenologist's first slip-up. After all, hadn't he fitted out Madame Courtois' little run-down winery with conical stainless steel vats – bizarre-looking things, copied, if you please, from medieval drawings? Didn't he also claim that the old, traditional chestnut-wood casks used in every cellar in the region gave the wine an acrid, dried-out flavour? He'd thrown all of his out in one go and replaced them with oak casks! The last straw came when he picked up all the top medals for the very first Bourgueil he ever made.

'Those blasted medals I won in my first year didn't exactly make me friends in the region! And then there were the bankers, who simply couldn't understand that I didn't want to sell my 1981 vintage "hot" from the winepress. It was a severe, unyielding vintage, and I knew it would need a few years of bottle-age before it softened out and became more amiable. I wanted to keep it for a few years rather than sell a tart young wine at a low price. Looking back, those days were really tough; we lived on next to nothing.'

But, as time went by, even the most jealous characters in the village had to admit that Pierre-Jacques was not such a bad chap after all, and that the gold medals he'd won were well-earned and not due to underhand bribes, as rumour would have it. Slowly but surely Pierre-Jacques' friendliness and natural generosity worked its charm on everyone. Even one or two of the most recalcitrant had to change their minds when they had to ask the new oenologist for advice on saving a vat from turning into vinegar. Despite his fifteen-hour working day, Pierre-Jacques was always ready to give a helping hand and to sort out some of his neighbours' haphazard vinifications.

'It's only natural to help your friends, whether they're wine producers or importers. I do it not only for their sakes, but also because of my love for the Loire Valley wines.'

One day a young wine-waiter from Bordeaux decided it was time he learnt something about Loire wines. 'As far as this young man's experience went,' Pierre-Jacques recalls, 'wines from the Loire region were served on only two kinds of occasion: it was either Muscadet when oysters were ordered, or Sancerre for American tourists! However, it was encouraging that he'd made the effort to come and see what was happening in Bourgueil. Not many wine waiters from Bordeaux would bother.'

Pierre-Jacques let the young man taste his wines, including the 1981, the vintage that had been underestimated by his bankers. A few years on, it now showed astonishing structure and elegance. He also uncorked his 1982 – a sensual feast – and then his other vintages. But the tasting session had only just begun. He couldn't let the man from Bordeaux go home with no idea of the Loire's other wine regions. Clasping a big old rusty key, he headed down to his personal cellar. The Druets by now were living in one of those typical old low-lying Loire houses made out of white chalk called tufa that softens with age.

He returned to the dining-room with a number of bottles under his arm. He and his guest were now fully equipped to set off on a long journey down the river Loire, starting with a dry Savennières, followed by a little detour via the luscious sweet whites from the

Coteaux du Layon. Heading on upstream towards Vouvray and Montlouis, they tasted the extraordinary number of ways the Chenin grape can express itself. It's like a chameleon, transforming itself to soak up the taste of the schistous stones in Savennières and the chalkiness in the Montlouis, and bursting forth with concentrated sweetness in the best vintages in Vouvray.

Then they moved on to the reds. From Anjou to Chinon, and from Bourgueil to Saumur-Champigny, the Cabernet Franc reveals a split personality. Treated with a thirst-quenching lightness by the producers in Saumur, it yields its most seductive fruitiness within its first few years; handled like a Bordeaux by some producers in Chinon and Bourgueil, it holds some stunning surprises back for decades. Towards midnight the wine waiter left the Druets, impressed with the quality and immense diversity of wines from the Loire. But Pierre-Jacques realises there is still a lot of work to be done to get the message across to wine drinkers that the Loire vineyards no longer produce syrupy rosés and over-perfumed sweetish whites, as they did between the Wars.

Nestling into the hillside just below his house is Pierre-Jacques' latest investment: the beginnings of a new spacious winery of his own design, which will eventually house his famous conical steel vats.

Pierre-Jacques got the idea for these when he was reading about how wine was made in the Middle Ages and came across an engraving which showed vinification vats that were narrower at the top than at the bottom. Compared with today's cylindrical vats, this ancient design has the brilliant advantage of compressing the 'cap' thus facilitating a better extraction of colour and tannin.

Pierre-Jacques chose to build his winery on a slope and on two levels, so that instead of using electric pumps to transfer his wines from one vat to another, he can make as much use as possible of gravity. He firmly believes that the less you pump a wine, the better it tastes. The new building will be used mainly during the wine's fermentation, and perhaps to stock his bottled wine. But this ultra-modern annexe will not in any way replace his deep cellar carved into the tufa chalk.

'I shall go on barrel-ageing my wines in these wonderful dark, damp labyrinths. Few wine-producing regions are fortunate enough to have natural cellars that provide perfect temperature and humidity for ageing wine throughout the year.'

One day, Pierre-Jacques invited me to a rather special tasting he had organised at his friend Edmond's cellar. I was in a particularly happy mood that day as I drove out of Bourgeuil uphill along the narrow tracks which thread their way through the vineyards of Grand Mont. The Grand Mont hillock overlooking Bourgueil makes wines for long-keeping. The soil is very heavy, and the mixture of clay and chalk produces the most structured and long-lived wines of the appellation. The idea of the tasting was to make our way gently back to the beginning of the century. But, before we reached Edmond's cellar, we stopped off at Pierre-Jacques' to taste his latest wine.

'This year, I decided for the first time to produce a small amount of Bourgueil Rosé. I let the juice and grape skins macerate together one night – a method called a *saignée d'une nuit* (literally, the bleeding of one night). It gives the wine just enough fruitiness and colour to remain light and frivolous. Then I aged it in oak casks for a few months, just long enough to soften its sharp corners and round out the wine.'

I couldn't quite imagine Pierre-Jacques producing frivolous wines. I was so used to tasting young, tannic, severe reds straight from his casks that this new departure was most intriguing. It turned out to be an enchantingly dry rosé, tasting of soft, ripe summer fruit – a wine just waiting to be drunk.

'You can drink this in the sun at lunchtime and you won't get a headache. It's so light in alcohol that it won't knock you out for the rest of the day, and it contains hardly any sulphites. I fermented it in large oak casks almost three times as big as the ones used in Bordeaux. They are more cumbersome to handle, but I find they give less of a vanilla-oaky flavour to the wine and enable the wine's own fresh fruitiness to express itself unhindered.'

Edmond Magnan was waiting for us in his cellar just a few minutes away from Pierre-Jacques'. Magnan used to be a football player, and is still sprightly although he is well over seventy. He now rents out some of his vineyard to Pierre-Jacques. I had been looking forward to tasting his vintage wines for a long time. They would give me some idea of what Pierre-Jacques' wines would taste like a hundred years hence.

Edmond poured us each a glass of his 1986, just to get us in the right mood before setting off on our 'time-journey'. It was the first and the last wine we were to spit out that evening. Once we had cast adrift from the time-tunnel, the wines were far too historic just to be assessed clinically and spat out. We headed for the 1950s, stopping briefly over the 1961 – a treasure saved from the frosts. When we felt at home with the 1955 – still surprisingly youthful, and with all its wits about it – we steered towards the 1947, where a long halt awaited us. This is considered *the* vintage of the century, and its fruitiness showed no sign of fatigue. As we savoured the wine, Edmond told us that back in 1948 the postman, the road-worker and the policeman had all been well aware of the quality of the vintage. Every time they passed by Edmond's cellar they would stop off, have a glass of wine, and then conveniently leave something behind. When they returned, Edmond would, of course, offer them another glass of the 1947. *Politesse oblige.*

'Between the three of them, they polished off an entire cask of the '47 over a year,' Edmond recalled, laughing. 'And that's not counting what the mushroom-pickers got through. They used to work in a network of cellars directly underneath mine, and would appear "for a chat" as soon as they heard my footsteps.'

After this monumental wine, we cast off gently towards 1933. It was still fairly deep in colour and had lingering autumnal aromas of undergrowth and game entrails. Edmond then disappeared to the back of his cellar and returned holding a bottle in a horizontal position, so as not to disturb the sediment. It was a 1928. He hadn't tasted it for at least ten years and wasn't sure if it would still be any good. It turned out to be the triumph of the evening. An anthology specimen, with fantastically complex aromas.

The evening finished very late. Our little group finally dispersed joyfully, having told each other our life histories and promised to go on another journey together. Next time we would venture further afield, towards the last century. Pierre-Jacques, his eyes twinkling with happiness, said a few last wise words as we left: 'Oeonology courses don't explain the most important thing about wine: the intimate understanding of a particular *terroir*. Only time and our elders can teach us that.'

Pierre-Jacques Druet
La Ferme
BP No. 1
Benais
37140 Bourgueil
Tel: 47.97.39.33

UK IMPORTERS/DISTRIBUTORS

Adnams Wine Merchants
The Crown
High Street
Southwold
Suffolk 1P18 6DP
tel: 0502 724222

Anthony Byrne Fine Wines
88 High Street
Ramsey
Cambs PE17 1BS
tel: 0487 814555

Justerini & Brooks Ltd
61 St James's Street
London SW1
tel: 071 493 8721

Morris & Verdin Ltd
28 Churton Street
London SW1V 2LP
tel: 071-630 8888

Yapp Producers Plc
The Old Brewery
Mere
Wilts BA12 6DY
tel: 0747 860423/860017

Jules Mabileau

I O W E M Y first serious trip to the Loire Valley to my friend Michel Bettane, the wine journalist. He was horrified to find I still hadn't visited the vineyards of Touraine and suggested we spend a weekend putting this right.

It was Easter, and the days were wonderfully bright – with that intense luminosity you often find in the Loire. We lunched in a bistro in Chinon, off local rillettes, bread and a glass of Breton. The Breton vine, better known today as the Cabernet Franc, originally came from Bordeaux, where it is still grown. In the Loire, however, it has been known as the Breton since the sixteenth century – Rabelais referred to it as 'Ce bon vin breton' – because it came to the region by boat via the Breton port of Nantes (in medieval times, Nantes was an important centre for wine distribution to the non-viticultural regions of France and Europe).*

Over coffee, Michel glanced at the local paper and noticed an advertisement for the annual wine fair in Bourgueil.

'Wonderful! We couldn't have come at a better time,' he said. Wine fairs have the same effect on him as summer sales have on some of my friends.

A wine fair at the Loire is in many ways much the same as a wine fair anywhere else in France: a green field becomes a showroom for

---

* *Histoire de la vigne et du vin en France des origines au XIXᵉ siècle*, by Roger Dion (Paris, 1959), Chapter IV.

shining agricultural machinery where erratic bursts from loud-speakers deafen visitors with the usual announcements of lost children, and there's plenty of candy-floss and laughter. The wine tasting is usually held in enormous chalk caves. These caves, originally hollowed out to provide blocks of tufa to build the local châteaux, are now used for making and ageing wine, and also for growing mushrooms; some of them are even converted into dwellings.

At the Bourgueil wine fair, two ranges of shelves are fixed against the chalk wall and each producer lines up a few bottles of his own wine and props up a hand-painted sign with his name on it. The fair is open to all. The entry ticket comes with a wine-tasting glass, and brokers, wine merchants and restaurateurs, as well as weekend strollers, are free to taste the hundred or so different wines on show. The Bourgueil fair has a medieval feeling about it: groups of people cluster here and there around a producer, tasting, chatting and occasionally spitting on the ground. The producers look forward to this event as much as everyone else. It's the one day of the year when they can freely observe their neighbours' business dealings, taste their rivals' wine and scrutinise their clients. In this festive rural atmosphere, there is always a touch of small-town jealousy in the air. It adds to the charm.

Before nightfall, after spending the whole afternoon in the cool dark of the cave tasting the latest vintages, we set off to Saumur. We chose a cross-country route so that we could take a close look at the vineyards as we drove along. We had reached the flat alluvial plain of Saint-Nicolas-de-Bourgueil when suddenly Michel slammed on the brakes. He'd spotted a vineyard full of old knotted wines. I realised right away that there was little chance of our leaving the area until we'd found the owner of the 'antique' roots.

We eventually found our man at La Taille, a hamlet between Saint-Nicolas-de-Bourgueil and the river Loire. We had been told in the village that his name was Mabileau, but were soon to discover that our M. Mabileau shared his surname with almost every other family in the hamlet. From that day on, to avoid confusion, I was to refer to 'our man' by his Christian name, Jules.

An old dog barked in a lazy way to warn of our arrival. Madame Mabileau, peeling the vegetables for the evening soup, peeped through the curtains to see who was in the courtyard. Eventually, a medium-sized man in his early fifties with extraordinarily limpid blue eyes emerged wearing a funny old baseball cap. He looked at us suspicously and grumbled to himself, annoyed at being disturbed. He obviously thought we'd come to a buy a cubitainer of wine ('cubitainers' are large plastic containers, holding five to twenty litres, used for selling wine in bulk for everyday drinking).

He was even less happy when, instead, we asked if we could taste the wine made from the old vineyard we had driven past. But, realising it wasn't going to be easy to get rid of us, he handed us a glass tumbler each, then he reached resignedly for his laddder and pipette, and slowly eased himself up to the top of a cement vat. The winery, which looked more like a wooden hangar, had a makeshift, haphazard look about it, and we began to think that maybe the wine wouldn't be that great after all. One sip was all we needed to dispel our fears. Jules' Saint-Nicolas-de-Bourgueil, whether tasted from cement vats or wooden casks, revealed an astonishing finesse and nobility.

Over the years, as I've got to know Jules, I've discovered that he shares these qualities. Perhaps they have something to do with the instinctive and profound respect he has for his land. There's not a square inch that he doesn't know by heart. He started ploughing it when he left school at the age of eleven 'and-a-half', and has only ever left the village twice – once to do his military service, and once when he went on a day's outing to the seaside.

'Holidays? I don't know what you're talking about,' he answered roughly, irritated that there can be such a gap between town and country dwellers. 'I've never even taken a weekend off. If I'm not around, who do you think will prune the vines, rack the wine, pick the asparagus? Asparagus doesn't wait for you to come back from your weekend. During the season it's got to be picked every day.'

During his father's lifetime, the Mabileaus had a little of everything: wheat, cows, hens, vines, a vegetable garden, fruit trees, and, of course, the two plough-horses. Jules' job was to look after the vines and take care of the horses. It was only when he got married in 1952, at the age of twenty-four, that he was finally allowed to start making a few decisions.

Ever since he was a young boy, he had enjoyed tending the vines and helping make the wine, though at the time wine was produced only as a means of making ends meet. Apart from a barrel a year which was bottled and set aside for home consumption, it was sold in bulk as soon as possible. Each spring, a broker would come to collect a few samples for the big *négociant* houses. Jules doesn't have particularly fond memories of this middleman.

'Bribery was the only way to make sure the brokers would come back to us with a firm order. They took cash from us, but they earned at least as much again in commissions from the *négociants*. Money was easy for them. But we farmers had to work our guts out to survive. Until my parents died, we all lived under the same roof – parents, children and grandchildren – with no prospect of earning enough money to buy a house of our own.'

The soil around La Taille is poor, as is all the low-lying land around Saint-Nicolas-de-Bourgueil; so poor that even fruit trees can't get enough nourishment and die after a few years. The thin alluvial topsoil is only about thirty centimetres deep, and to prove to me how unpropitious the subsoil is, Jules once dug up shovel after shovel of little else but small walnut-sized stones. 'The vine's the only plant that could possibly survive in it,' he said with a mixture of pride and admiration.

'The flat lands around here are particularly prone to frost. Take 1945. I remember it was May the eighth, a national holiday, and we had a very severe frost. Instead of making around ten or eleven thousand litres of wine, our three hectares of vines produced only one hundred litres. I can't imagine how we'd have survived that year if we'd had to pay back a loan on a tractor or a refrigerator. As it was, in 1945 and 1946 we had even less income than usual and lived off just what the farm produced.'

1961 is another year Jules remembers. That was when the horses retired from working life and he took out a loan for the first time – to buy a tractor. It was a big step to take in those days, because wines from the Loire valley were still very difficult to sell. The arrival of the tractor didn't even leave Jules with more free time on his hands.

'The nearest thing we ever got to being on holiday was during the grape harvest. It was the only time of the year when the villagers got together to help each other out. We'd work a couple of days in a neighbour's vineyard, a few days at another, and so on until all the grapes were harvested. Everyone was out to have a good time. We had breakfast and lunch together, we dined and danced together, and there were three village balls a week. Even the older generation stayed up until eleven o'clock at night singing and dancing.' This was considered very late for people who started work when the sun rose and usually went to bed at nightfall.

It was during the harvest that land transactions used to take place. The older men, realising they didn't have as much energy as before, would intimate that they were ready to sell off some of their property. 'But nowadays,' laments Jules, 'even neighbours and complete strangers buy plots of land behind your back!' Further evidence for him that we have come to the end of an era.

Another subject that annoys him are those *sacré* social-security charges.

'Grape-picking isn't what it used to be. The Ministry of Employment won't believe that people come to pick grapes to help us, just for the fun of it. If we don't watch out, the civil service will end up running everything.'

Jules was able to pay the pickers an hourly wage, but he couldn't afford to double the sum involved so as to pay social-security charges too. So, a couple of years ago, he set about hiring a mechanical harvester.

In any case, at over sixty, he thinks he's worked long enough, and has already split up his six hectares and given them to his two sons. Over a number of generations these divisions and sub-divisions will have at least one main advantage.

'Our property is divided up into fifteen small plots scattered across the appellation, some on a tufa subsoil, others on a stony one. The geographic division makes the work a bit more compli-

39

cated, but at least it means that if there's a patch of frost on one plot, there's a chance that those located on the other side of the village may escape.'

The largest section of Jules' vineyard was planted by his father in 1939 on lands that have grown vines for centuries. It was those vines that Michel Bettane spotted. In 1970, Jules replanted another part of the vineyard, replacing tired vines too old to produce grapes. Two further plots were replanted a couple of years ago.

At the last planting, instead of using vines grafted from the old vineyard, Jules used the new clonal-selected varieties. These vines, with identical genes, were developed by the National Institute for Agricultural Research and are produced from super-performing, disease-free grafts.

The advantages of this method are that it produces high yields and saves time – the old method meant going through the vineyard year by year marking out the best vines and then getting a nurseryman to graft the individual cuttings. As Jules warns, however, high yields are often achieved at the expense of quality – which is ultimately reflected in the wine's price.

'This last time round we'd no choice but to plant clonal-selected vines,' he says. 'They're the only plants the nurserymen are prepared to sell nowadays. At least we shan't be able to complain about low yields any more! But the younger generation want the best of both worlds. They want to harvest huge quantities and at the same time sell their wine at a high price. I suppose they'll learn from their mistakes sooner or later. But if they don't react soon, the wines from the Loire will all taste the same because they'll come from identical grapes produced from identical clones.'

Jules makes use of modern oenology twice a year, when he drops off a sample of wine for analysis at the local laboratory. The first trip to the laboratory is to make sure that the malolactic fermentation is finished.

The day malolactic fermentation was finally understood Jules must have heaved a sigh of relief. The discovery of the workings of this so-called fermentation – which is, in fact, the transformation by bacteria of malic acid (the one found in green apples) into lactic acid (the one found in milk) – set the wine producer free from a whole web of old wives' tales.

The most widely believed theory was that wine started to 'ferment' again in spring in sympathy with the rising sap in the vines. If a wine vat didn't start bubbling again after the winter, the wine grower thought someone must have cast a spell on it.

The second trip to the oenologist takes place later in the year just before bottling. This is to decide the amount of sulphur dioxide that needs to be added to the vat. Sulphur dioxide acts as a much-needed antiseptic. Only a small quantity is added so that it affects neither the taste nor the smell of a wine; but enough must be present to halt the development of unwanted yeasts and bacteria.

'Not so long ago, *négociants* used to take my wine as it was. Now they are only interested in buying a wine if it's been filtered. They don't want the consumer to buy a bottle with the slightest deposit in it. I hate filtering a wine because each time it's clarified through a filter, it loses some of its character. I've always thought that wines are the opposite of women. The less you touch them, the better they are!'

He also can't stand the feeling that his work is increasingly run by city-dwelling bureaucrats who now even prescribe the amount of time a wine takes to ferment.

'In the old days,' he says, 'if a vat took a long time to finish fermenting we just put it down to its being a slow starter and that was that. Today, in order to have the *appellation contrôlée* label, the wine must have completed its fermentation by the time official samples are taken at the end of the summer following the harvest. So, what do you do if you have a "lazy" vat? The answer is, you call in the oenologist who will gear the stuff into action by giving it a shot of selected yeasts. But if you'd left the wine to finish its fermentation at its own pace, the taste would have been quite different.'

There is now a wide range of selected yeasts on the market. Some work better in low temperatures, some when there is just a small amount of sugar left in the grape juice to be fermented. They are useful in getting a problem vat going again. But selected yeasts give a wine a different flavour from that which results if the natural yeasts present on the grape skin are allowed to do their job. Differences in the taste of wines from the same village will obviously be reduced if the same selected yeast has been used.

The first time I met Jules Mabileau, I was struck by the pure 'expression' of his wines. I promised myself that one day I would help promote their simplicity and nobility.

The opportunity arose a couple of years later when I was about to open the Legrand Filles et Fils wine shop in Paris. I couldn't take any time off to go to La Taille to taste the 1981 vintage, so I 'phoned and asked for a sample to be sent.

It must have been the first time Jules had been asked to send a sample bottle by mail. A few days later, I received a bottle of Saint-Nicolas-de-Bourgueil carefully wrapped in the local Touraine newspaper. I couldn't wait to taste it. Instead of laying the sample down to rest for a few weeks as I usually would, I uncorked it as soon as it arrived and tasted it with M. Legrand. To my great relief, the red fruit aromas, and the elegance and uprightness that I had often enjoyed in the past, were still there.

It was a perfect reflection of the *terroir* from which it came. For a mere 23F (£2.30) a bottle, one could happily either drink it right away or lay it down for another twenty years.

Jules was still rather doubtful when I placed my first order. How could he be sure he would ever be paid? He had never sold to a wine shop before, let alone to a shop in Paris. Finally, he made up his mind and dispatched the wine. His Saint-Nicolas-de-Bourgueil soon became one of my customers' favourites.

Our 'business' relationship led to a long and delightful correspondence. Jules' replies always began 'Monsieur'. It was only after a few years that he came to terms with the fact that the buyer was a woman. A lot of effort went into these carefully handwritten letters. He used unusual yet powerful images to describe the countryside and the surprises nature had sprung that season. If one of my orders coincided with the asparagus-picking season, I knew that I'd just have to wait until the season was over. Jules never liked bottling in a hurry and, no matter how urgently the wine was needed, he would finish the picking first.

When we got to know each other better, I decided to tell him what I thought about the appearance of his bottles. The bottle-cap, or capsule, made of thick, nasty red plastic, was ugly and impractical. Several restaurateurs liked the wine but nevertheless refused to put it on their wine list because they found it impossible to get to the cork. But Jules stubbornly refused to buy new machinery to fit on tin-foil capsules instead of plastic ones. He claimed it was far too expensive an investment and, after all, it was what was in the bottle that was important and not the packaging.

Then I tried to sort out another problem. He used the same label as everyone else in the village. It was brown and red, dull, and meant to look vaguely like a piece of burnt parchment. The equally unattractive matching label on the neck of the bottle had at least one virtue: the vintage date was legible. However, faced with Jules' resigned silence, and afraid I might have hurt his pride, I dropped the subject.

Some time later, when I was travelling through the Loire, the Mabileaus invited me, for the first time, to share their lunch. Château-owners in Bordeaux give luncheons every day – it has become part of their job, a well-polished public-relations exercise. But, to the Loire, the wiles of PR haven't yet filtered through and invitations, when they come, do so straight from the heart. This all made the Mabileaus' lunch, the chicken plucked fresh for the *coq au vin*, taste even better!

In their white tufa house, where all the living space is taken up by the kitchen and the bedroom, Jules proudly showed me the new label which he'd designed himself. It depicted two winding roads leading from Saint-Nicolas-de-Bourgueil to his house. The whole scene was lit up by a large sun. And he'd drawn another one on the neck label, as if he felt the world could do with an extra sun to bring some warmth back to men's hearts.

Jules Mabileau
La Taille
Saint-Nicolas-de-Bourgueil
37140 Bourgueil
tel: 47.97.77.92

Nicolas Joly

*C*URNONSKY, the revered French food critic of the
1920s, once wrote that France produced five great wines.
His list comprised Yquem, Montrachet, Château-Grillet,
Château-Chalon and the Coulée de Serrant. I had tasted this last
wine on a few occasions; it is unlike any other dry white in the
world. But despite my ten years in the wine trade, I had never
visited the domaine.

My first meeting with Nicolas Joly, owner of the small, walled
vineyard overlooking the Loire, began in somewhat unusual circumstances. As I approached the domaine, a few kilometres south-
east of Angers, I started to think about the last bottle of Coulée
de Serrant I'd tasted. The narrowness of the winding road, which
runs through the charming village of Epiré and crosses the Savennières appellation, didn't stop me from concentrating on the aromas
of that splendid 1964. The memory was almost as good as the real
thing: that aristocratic old-gold colour, the wonderful aroma –
tight, dry and flinty yet with a taste so full and rich in the flavours
of honey, gingerbread and lime-blossom. But suddenly my daydream was interrupted. The car was in a deep ravine, and had
come to an abrupt stop against a tree trunk.

I managed to clamber out of the almost vertical Renault and
continued on foot. The Clos de la Coulée de Serrant was just a
few hundred yards away, but I soon realised the extent of my bad

luck. I had managed to crash near the only domaine I knew of where horses were used to plough the vineyard – in all probability, there would be no tractor to pull the car out of the ditch!

Nicolas Joly, a handsome man in his early forties, greeted my problem and my gloom with equal serenity. 'The last visitor to get stuck in a ditch here,' he observed, 'was Louis the Fourteenth. And though he was particularly fond of the wine from the Coulée de Serrant, he, too, is said to have been "out of humour" that day.'

In no time at all, the car was extracted from its muddy ditch with the help, much to my surprise, of a brand new caterpillar tractor, skilfully manoeuvred by a domaine employee. He was obviously used to transporting cumbersome objects, for Nicolas Joly has scattered a number of menhirs – pre-historic monumental stones – here and there about his domaine.

'It may strike you as peculiar,' said M. Joly, 'but I became convinced that a few menhirs dotted about the vineyard, and placed above the confluences of underground streams, would remove negative elements from the soil and restore the general harmony.'

Menhirs are apparently as easy to find as discarded gas stoves. 'I simply put an advert in the local paper saying "Menhirs wanted". The following week an old man 'phoned to say he had some "lovely pieces". As if,' Nicolas Joly went on, laughing heartily, 'he was talking about jewellery or antiques!'

The Coulée de Serrant is, to my mind, among the two or three most beautiful vineyards in France. Steep hills overlook a majestic sweep of the Loire where it is swollen by its tributary, the Maine. Large islands scattered in midstream look strangely transient, as if awaiting a signal to cast off and drift down with the slow yet powerful current to the sea. The Coulée de Serrant's slopes, covered with fragments of crumbling schist, which are sizzling hot in summer, seem to tumble down towards the river as if unable to resist the lure of its cool tranquillity. Autumn brings heavy morning mists that float up the hillside and seem to envelop each bunch of grapes separately. By late afternoon, the mist evaporates, leaving an irridescent glow on the pink, sandy riverbanks.

For centuries this view was incongruously dominated by a fortified feudal castle. But in the eighteenth century, the castle made way for an enchanting country mansion which fits in very much better with the landscape. This was the place that Nicolas' father, a surgeon from Angers, fell in love with, a love which his son shares completely.

'One weekend in the 1950s my father came across this enchanting manor house with its breathtaking view over the Loire. He was so taken by it that he asked, on the off-chance, if it was for sale. Not surprisingly, the startled owner answered that it was not. But a week later the 'phone rang. The proprietor said he was prepared to sell after all. Almost overnight, my parents moved in and became the proud owners not only of a house they adored but also of a domaine. It included the Coulée de Serrant, a seven-hectare, single-varietal vineyard, originally planted by monks in the twelfth century, and a further four-hectare vineyard, the Roche-aux-Moines. The property soon took up all my parents' time and, as my father would say, it was more costly than a mistress.'

'In 1959, when my parents moved in, the vineyard was losing money. It started to break even only after my mother had devoted twenty years of her life to it. She worked tirelessly to restore the Coulée de Serrant's pre-War reputation. Much of her energy went into developing the commercial side of the business, which she still deals with today.'

Madam Joly's painstaking labours paid off. The Coulée de Serrant wine is now stocked in the cellars of just about every three-star restaurant in the Michelin guide.

The only grape variety planted at the Coulée de Serrant is the Chenin. It is, without doubt, the most noble white grape of the Loire. After a number of years in bottle, its wines burst forth with delightful, lingering aromas. But the recent trend for quick-maturing, easy-to-drink wines means that the Chenin grape has fallen rather out of favour. Many wine drinkers, opting for young, aromatic dry whites, go for the Sauvignon grape with its straight-forward nose of freshly cut grass. This is good news for the more patient Chenin-lovers: the price of Vouvrays, Coteaux du Layons and other Chenin wines are still well below their true market value.

Nicolas Joly devotes his whole life to growing the Chenin grape, though when he was younger no-one, least of all his parents, would have dreamed that he would later become fascinated by agriculture. He majored in Business Studies at Columbia University, and then worked in the investment research department of a merchant bank in New York. All the while, however, a deep desire to be closer to nature was growing within him.

What sparked off this yearning? Was it, perhaps, the endless business meetings in smoke-filled rooms? Or the hunting and fishing weekends in the wilds of Canada? Whatever the cause, by the time his father died, Nicolas was sure enough of his leanings to know exactly what he wanted to do.

'In 1976 I was transferred to London and worked in the City. One day the bank's senior partner called me into his office and told me that I was going to be promoted. I thanked him profusely, and announced with great relish that I had, in fact, decided to leave the bank and go back to France to tend my family's vines. I had to use a more subtle approach to convey this decision to my wife. She's the daughter of a German diplomat, and a city-lover at heart. She thought she'd married a successful City banker and was now suddenly confronted with the fact that she was really living with an earthy *paysan*!'

The young Joly family moved to the Coulée de Serrant to the only other building on the property, a large house originally dating back to the twelfth century and rebuilt by monks in the fifteenth century. Nestling in the hollow of a little valley, surrounded by lush green fields where geese, ducks, horses and even cows graze peacefully, it has a strangely idyllic and almost English feel about it.

Nicolas had come back to help his widowed mother run the property. At first, he did little else but observe how the vineyard was run. He watched, incredulously, as the workers ploughed huge quantities of chemicals into the soil. Later, he listened with increasing amusement to the representatives' sales-pitch for their various agricultural products: 'With this weedkiller, your vineyard will be spotlessly clean – it destroys anything that tries to grow between the vines.' 'Take my word for it, this insecticide doesn't kill bees – it's selective . . .'

Although he knew little about vineyards, Nicolas Joly already had a feeling that a wine's *typicité*, or fundamental local character, was due to its soil and subsoil. A vine with a root system going deep down into the soil will feed its fruit on the minerals and trace elements it finds there, thus giving the grape its unique character. But in soils where the natural bacterial life has been killed off, roots have little incentive to develop. Instead they remain near the surface of the soil and lazily await their 'intravenous drip' – a regular dose of fertilisers.

Despite the Wall Street banker's first 'green' symptoms, however, no-one could have imagined that Nicolas would eventually become a faithful disciple of Rudolf Steiner, the turn-of-the-century Austrian philosopher and father of biodynamic farming.

'One winter's day, in 1981, I was browsing in my favourite Paris bookshop in the rue de Seine and I came across a book on biodynamic farming. I took it with me on a skiing holiday, but forgot all about it until the weather broke. Then, stuck indoors, I started to read it, and soon I couldn't put it down. It was full of common sense, and dealt with many questions I'd been unable to answer since I'd started working on the domaine. When I'd finished reading it, I knew there was an alternative to chemical fertilisers and weedkillers.'

Back at the Coulée de Serrant, Nicolas Joly started to read the rest of Rudolf Steiner's books. Steiner, a student of Goethe and a thinker in cosmic terms – perhaps best known in England for his theory of education – invented a new form of farming based on balance and respect for nature. 'I've read and re-read a number of Steiner's books, but I can't say they're any easier to understand the second time round,' Nicolas Joly admits. 'Nevertheless, with every reading, I become more fascinated.'

Nicolas started to carry out a few biodynamic experiments of his own. 'The process was completely crazy and fraught with beginners' problems,' he recalls. 'In some ways it's rather like homeopathy in that microscopic doses are used. I didn't know of anyone else who was involved in biodynamics, so I had to make up the "medicine" myself.

'One of my basic vineyard treatments involves mixing various natural ingredients in a stag's bladder, which then has to be buried deep in the ground for a few months and later brought up to air for a further few more months. At first, the farm-workers looked at me as if I was possessed by the devil! To add to the eccentricity of it all, each stage has to be carried out at specific times, in accordance with the movements of the planets.

'The final phase consists of taking a minute quantity of the contents of the stag's bladder, and "dynamising" it. First of all, a single measure of the substance is diluted in nine times its volume of water, giving what is called a D1. Then a measure of this new solution is diluted again in nine times *its* volume of water, which produces a D2. The process continues until a D8 is obtained. The D8 solution is then sprayed on the vines. The initial product has by this time been diluted down to one millionth of its original strength.

'What's so disturbing about biodynamics to modern man's scientific way of thinking is that often, the more a solution is diluted, the greater its effect! Current experiments on the "memory" of water may eventually shed light on the matter and give some much-needed scientific backing to biodynamic theories.'

To the uninitiated, this spraying of a watered-down concoction on the vines might seem a disturbing mixture of witchcraft and homeopathy. Nicolas Joly was, in fact, about to give up his complicated and time-consuming tests when he heard that a wine producer in the nearby Saumur area had been running a biodynamic vineyard for the past twenty-five years. 'I went straight round to see him,' Nicolas recalls. 'His vines looked radiant. I scooped some soil up in my hands: it was moist, light as flour, and smelt wonderfully, profoundly earthy. It seemed truly alive and healthy.'

Nicolas Joly is now convinced that the biodynamic method is

the best. Once a year, he organises a weekend seminar at the domaine. The guest speaker is invariably the German specialist, Mrs Thunn, Europe's greatest expert on the subject. Biodynamic farming is slowly arousing more and more interest among farmers throughout Europe, and some food shops now even have a special 'biodynamic' section. Scientists are also beginning to work on biodynamics. As yet, no-one has been able to prove scientifically that planetary movements have a direct influence on the quality of a crop, but researchers are baffled by the unquestionable superiority in flavour and shelf-life of biodynamic food products.

Getting farm-workers to gaze at the stars to find out their week's work schedule, however, isn't always easy. 'The man who used to run the vineyard here,' Nicolas recounts, 'had already lived through one agricultural revolution in his lifetime – the introduction of chemical fertilisers and weedkillers. He looked upon biodynamics as a huge leap backwards. When he saw that I was firmly set on it, he left! However, the current team are with me one hundred per cent. Their average age is between forty and fifty, and they've always lived in the country. As children, they used to listen to their grandmothers handing down old sayings such as "Only sow corn after full moon", so they tend to understand my way of thinking.

'Each of the farm-hands carries out his work according to the astral calendar. Today, for example, we are in Sagittarius, a heat sign, a good time to plough. But, in a couple of days' time, we'll be moving into another sign, and then it will be a complete waste of time to plough. We shall be under the new influence for ten days. The farm-workers know this and accept it. Sometimes, in accordance with the astral movements, we have to work the weekend; at other times we might have to start spraying the vines at 5 a.m. or at 10 p.m. But as soon as the calendar allows it, the workers know they can take a few days off. It's not a nine to five job, but we usually manage to work things out to everyone's satisfaction.'

Once biodynamic farming has been started on a 'modern' soil, it apparently takes a full seven years for the earth to recover its own natural balance. But, after only five years of biodynamic treatment, Nicolas' vines already look exceptionally healthy.

A strong vine planted in a wholesome soil acts as a repellent to outside aggressors. For instance, as the red spider, a typical vine pest, attacks only weak vines, it is totally unnecessary for Nicolas Joly to treat his vines against this parasite.

Despite the obviously healthy vines at the Coulée de Serrant, it didn't take long for wild rumours to spread. Some people said Nicolas Joly had finally gone off his rocker, and that the domaine's wines were no longer what they used to be. These gossipers should be forced, thirty years from now, to watch us drink the Coulée de Serrant currently being produced by Nicolas Joly.

'Our wine's biggest handicap is its incredible ageing capacity,' Nicolas Joly says, in deadly earnest. 'The wine can be drunk "on its fruit" within the first year or two, when the primary fruity aromas come through. Then it goes through an adolescent phase when it closes in on itself. Not the slightest pleasure can be got from drinking it. It only really comes into its own after about ten or twenty years of bottle-age.'

How, I ask myself, could the wine from Coulée de Serrant possibly be less good now than it used to be? The vines have never been tended with such care. The steepest slopes are ploughed by about the only piece of modern machinery on the property, the caterpillar tractor. The rest of the ploughing is left to the four elderly plough-horses which have worked on the domaine all their lives. They know each row of vines as well as they know their manager. (The purpose of ploughing is to cut off the lesser roots near the upper surface of the soil. The vine, unable to rely on shallow sources of supply, is forced to seek more complex nourishment from the main root burrowing deep down.)

Needless to say, the grapes are hand-picked. But the grape-pickers aren't just let loose on the vines and told to cut. They pick only the ripe bunches; the less ripe ones are left until the sun has completed its work. Over the harvest period, a grape-picker will probably pick his way through the same rows of vines about three times.

'If we have a particularly sunny autumn, we hold off picking until the grapes reach perfect maturity and are almost baked by the sun. The schistous soil is the vine's great ally. It always retains a little humidity but, most importantly, stores daytime heat and releases it back to the vines at night.'

October is the best month at the Coulée de Serrant. Early in the morning, a thick mist spreads up from the Loire and submerges the vineyard. This, followed by hot midday sunshine, produces ideal climatic conditions for the development of Botrytis cinerea. This miraculous fungus, more commonly known as 'noble rot', attacks the grapes and is responsible for producing – here as at Yquem – a golden grape juice, bursting with concentrated sugar.

'With top-quality grapes, you'd really have to work hard to make bad wine,' Nicolas Joly comments. 'As far as I'm concerned, the most nerve-wracking period is from the time that the buds first appear on the vines until the harvest. After that, it's plain sailing. My worries come to an end once all the ripe grapes are picked and are in the winery.' Unlike most winemakers, Nicolas Joly never has sleepless nights over the vinification.

Low yields are a key factor in producing concentrated wines. On average, the domaine yields are around 25 to 30 hl/ha. 'In 1988, we had eighteen hectolitres per hectare. That's one of our best vintages, along with 1978, 1989 and 1990. We didn't have to chaptalise, as the wine has a natural alcohol content of thirteen per cent and a lovely backbone of acidity. The only problem is that we'll have to wait a good twenty-five years before the 88s start to show themselves at their best.'

The vinification process at the Coulée de Serrant couldn't be simpler. In the vaulted white-washed cellars, lined with large, 600-litre wooden barrels, the grape juice bubbles away, fermenting at its own pace for about six months. Nothing is added. Selected yeasts may have the advantage of speeding up the fermentation process, but only at the expense of the wine's *typicité*.

'I hardly interfere with the wine at all,' says Nicolas. 'I rack it three times, and that's about all. Also, in order to even out the slight differences that may develop between one cask and another, I redistribute the contents of every three barrels among themselves. It's important that, as far as possible, all the bottles of a given vintage should taste the same. The Coulée de Serrant and the Roche-aux-Moines are, first and foremost, dry whites. The few bunches of grapes that have got "noble rot" are crushed with the rest of the harvest. They give the wine a rich texture. I don't want to start making special cuvées of sweet wine – it would only confuse our clientele, who expect our wine to be dry. In 1989, however, the weather was so exceptionally hot, and the grapes so full of sugar, that I couldn't resist vinifying a small cask of semi-sweet wine just to satisfy my own curiosity. But making sweet wines really isn't my business. I prefer to concentrate on dry wines.'

Most wine producers add a fining agent to their wine to help precipitate particles in suspension which otherwise might leave the wine looking a little cloudy or hazy. Fining agents range from egg-whites and skimmed milk to isinglass and bull's blood. They don't add any flavour to a wine but tend to thin its body. Nicolas Joly won't hear of fining. When asked why he doesn't go in for it, he answers: 'Why should I add eggs to my wine?' The only other process he applies to his wine is a light filter prior to bottling ... in accordance, of course, with planetary movements.

Most winegrowers have an almost instinctive desire to leave a mark on their soil. Nicolas Joly is no exception. He was, however, attracted by the most impossible piece of land, left fallow for very good reason for more than a century. It's the sort of slope that would normally be more attractive to a skier than to a farmer. Beside the stone wall boundary of the Coulée de Serrant is a steep slope stretching down to the Loire. And, as if the gradient weren't enough to make ploughing, among other things, difficult, the topsoil is full of the slate that is one of the ploughshare's worst enemies. But Nicolas Joly, with the help of his caterpillar tractors, decided against all odds that this was where he wanted to create 'his' vineyard. 'We started to clear the land – its local name is Bécherel – in 1985. By 1988, we had managed to plant just under one-and-a-half hectares. But we still have a couple more hectares to go. I had a most frustrating time trying to find the Chenin vines I wanted. Most nurseries nowadays supply only clonal-selected vines.'

Needless to say, Nicolas Joly would never plant clonal-selected vines. In his opinion, they not only produce far too great a yield, but their grapes are all stereotyped. With them, it would be impossible to obtain the richness and diversity of flavour that come from a large 'population' of vines that have adapted themselves over the years to the local climate and soil.

'It sounds crazy, but I finally had to call Michel Bettane, the wine journalist, in Paris. He knew of a nursery that sold "selection massale" reproduced from a wide variety of vines.'

Over the years, Nicolas Joly has paid little attention to his reputation as an eccentric. He couldn't help feeling vindicated, however, when he heard that some of France's greatest wine domaines were turning to biodynamic viticulture. Madame Bize-Leroy, co-owner of the most famous domaine in Burgundy, has turned to biodynamic farming in her own twenty-five-hectare Domaine Leroy. A handful of other eminent châteaux and domaines are now beginning to follow the same example.

Maybe the wine world, having gone through its 'modern' phase when white-coated oenologists and stainless steel vats were all the rage, is about to come full circle and pay attention, first and foremost, to the quality of its grapes.

Nicolas Joly
Clos de la Coulée de Serrant
49170 Savennières
tel: 41 72 22 32

NICOLAS JOLY

UK IMPORTERS/DISTRIBUTORS

Stapylton Fletcher Ltd
Haslemere
Sutton Road
Maidstone
Kent ME15 9NE
tel: 0622 691188

Georges Lepré

A *LOT OF* people dining in restaurants dread the moment when the wine waiter appears. They have an uneasy feeling they're about to be taken for a ride, a nagging suspicion that the sommelier is paid on a commission basis and so will always suggest the most expensive bottles on the list. An introduction to Georges Lepré, the sommelier at the Ritz in Paris, should help to dispel this idea.

There's never a dull moment with Georges Lepré. The air of authority that surrounds him is counterbalanced by a bubbling sense of humour. And so I was delighted when, at a wine-tasting in which I was taking part, I spotted his aquiline nose hovering over a glass. The tasting was organised by Peter Thustrup, a Paris-based wine dealer who specialises in rare vintages, and it was being held in honour of one of his clients. It so happened that this particular wine collector, a Japanese, had bought some exceptional bottles of Bordeaux: the usual list of *grands crus classés* headed by Mouton, Lafite, Latour and Margaux, but all dating back to 1869 – that is, to the pre-phylloxera period.

Unfortunately, we weren't invited to taste these wines – they were collectors' pieces! But Thustrup uncorked six classic wines for us to taste blind – a leisurely task compared with the usual marathon tastings of thirty wines or more. The ordeal lasted just over a quarter-of-an-hour. We were all very disciplined; none of us swapped notes. The only sounds, as we each tried to figure out the wines' origins, were short, sharp sniffs, muffled swillings and the scratching of pens.

For the fourth wine I wrote: 'Brick-orange in colour, showing signs of considerable age. Still austere on the nose but surprisingly perky for such an obviously old wine. Bordeaux, of course. In the mouth, the wine confirms its youthful impression. Full of ripe red fruit; undoubtedly a great vintage. The tannins are beginning to soften out, producing a velvety wine full of sensual pleasures. Plenty of lingering flavours which gradually fade away. I conclude that it must be a Médoc from the commune of Saint-Julien. It can't be a Margaux – it's not graceful enough. And it isn't forceful enough for a Pauillac. But the sample manages to combine a little of both these qualities. A Saint-Julien therefore – 1966 perhaps? No, a little older maybe. How about a 1961?'

Georges Lepré agreed with me up to a point. Bordeaux, of course, but he was convinced that it was more like a Graves than a Médoc ... Help – maybe I'd got it all wrong! My confidence vanished and I plunged my nose back into the glass.

Eventually, Peter Thustrup took pity on us and revealed the terrible truth. It wasn't a Bordeaux but a Burgundy – a Musigny 1961 from the Comte de Vogüé. I'd known better moments! Luckily, Georges Lepré didn't let me down. Until then he'd hardly said anything, apart from the fact that he didn't think it was a Médoc. He could easily have merely repeated that opinion. Instead, he was amused by the blunder. 'Once again the professional tasters get it all wrong!' he said. 'It just goes to show we should be a little more humble!'

Georges Lepré is a legendary figure. The extreme luxury of the Paris Ritz lends an aura of its own to those who work there, but Georges also has a distinction all his own. Some people even feel slightly apprehensive when they meet him for the first time. His name is often dropped at smart dinner parties in New York, Tokyo and Rome when guests, just back from Paris, are proud to quote his views on a recent Montrachet or to mention his undying admiration for the Mouton 1928.

The sober elegance of his perfectly tailored black suit tends to enhance the legend, but Georges Lepré is quick to put the diner at his ease. 'Wine waiters should never forget that a customer is here to enjoy his dinner, not to be intimidated.'

He sticks firmly to that simple principle, rarely grants interviews, and never lets his name be used for promotional purposes. Thus he remains free to say exactly what he thinks about whatever wine he wishes to discuss – veiling his more controversial views in suitably diplomatic language.

He loves his job, reigning over the cellars of the most famous hotel in the world. Every morning, at ten o'clock, he switches on his computer to check his stock of over 130,000 bottles, including some of France's oldest and most eminent wines. He has an army of specialists to help him run his empire. Twelve *cafetiers* work exclusively in the *cave du jour*, or day cellar, getting the ice-buckets ready and preparing the wine bottles ordered in the dining-rooms. Fifteen wine waiters work in the restaurant, and also cater to the needs of jet-setters in private dining-rooms and luxury suites.

Asked how he became one of the most celebrated wine waiters in the world, Georges answers modestly in his soft rolling accent from the French South West. 'I had a terribly ordinary start in life,' he says. Ordinary for him maybe . . .

He was born east of Bordeaux near the Côtes de Buzet, in a commune that produces a locally drunk wine called the Côtes du Brulhois. 'Wine was part of our daily life. At harvest-time, for example, all the children in the village were sent out to pick the grapes. It couldn't have been more ordinary.' His father was a cobbler, and, to this day, he recalls the heady smell of leather in his father's shop.

From an early age he wanted to be a cook, and left home to go on a training course in Toulouse. But, after he had passed his exams, he decided it was time to make a secret dream come true and become an opera singer! He signed on at the local academy of music and was soon singing duets with a charming young woman, who later became his wife.

Their meeting was a turning point in Georges Lepré's career.

He soon had to admit that his voice wasn't quite as magical as his wife's, and so returned to his first vocation and started work at the well-respected Grand Hôtel in Souillac. There, he did just about everything but cook. He worked at the reception desk, and later became head waiter.

One day, in the mid-1960s, some Canadians on a gastronomic tour of France came to the restaurant to enjoy the regional specialities of *cèpes* and *confits*. There they met Georges, and couldn't understand what such a talented person was doing buried away in the depths of the Périgord. As they left, they said they would mention his name to Raymond Oliver. They were dining at his restaurant in Paris that very evening, and claimed they knew him well.

Georges Lepré didn't pay much attention to the Canadians' enthusiastic promises. Any idea of working for Raymond Oliver seemed too fantastic. 'The name Raymond Oliver was out of this world to someone like me, stuck far away in the provinces,' Lepré recalls. 'At that time he was the only great chef in France. He was Bocuse, Guérard and Senderens all rolled into one.'

Some time later, however, Raymond Oliver was on holiday in Souillac and, tipped off by the Canadians, asked to meet Georges. Straightaway, he offered him a job as maître d'hôtel in his internationally known restaurant, Le Grand Véfour. Georges was overjoyed. 'I can remember saying to my fiancée: "I'll go, even if I have to pay to work there!"'

The Grand Véfour was then at the height of its fame. The intimate, romantic restaurant, with its glittering nineteenth-century decor, tucked away at one end of the gardens of the Palais Royal, was a temple of gastronomy. People came from all over the world to sample Oliver's cooking.

When Georges started his new job, the wine waiter, Philibert Henocq, was eighty-five years old. 'He was a sort of walking legend,' Georges recalls with affection. 'He only ever had two employers in his whole life. He worked as a wine waiter in a seaside hotel in Normandy until he was sixty-five. Then, at an age when most men retire, he moved to the Grand Véfour, and stayed there until he was eighty-nine. He was, without doubt, one of the greatest wine waiters ever.

'He never showed the wine list to clients, and no-one even dared to ask for it. As he approached each table, he glanced quickly at the diners, gauged the situation, and without a moment's hesitation decided what his clients were going to drink. No client ever dared contradict him – as a matter of fact, they loved the whole performance. He usually guessed exactly what they enjoyed drinking and, just as important, guessed how much they were prepared to spend.

After Philibert Henocq's death, Raymond Oliver asked Georges if he'd like to take over as wine waiter. Georges tried out Henocq's method a number of times. 'It was an utter disaster. I always ended up having to go and get the wine list and let the diners look at it. I realised then that, in this profession, age confers authority.'

Eventually, though, he found that the wine list itself could be a very useful tool. 'I could pick up clues about what a client wanted to drink just by the way he flipped through it. Some customers had a glazed look as they skipped through the pages, others avoided the Burgundies and made straight for the expensive older Bordeaux.'

It was under the guidance of Philibert Henocq, whom Georges regarded as a 'grandfather', that he had started to study wines seriously. In those days, visits to the vineyards took place in the restaurant wine cellar, corkscrew in hand! No-one actually went to the wine-producing regions. Travelling took up far too much time and money. Wine waiters were not, as they are now, invited to the great châteaux and domaines and treated as VIPs.

Georges Lepré started to read about wine, devouring book after book. As most of the better publications were in English, he killed two birds with one stone and learnt English at the same time. 'In our trade it's absolutely essential to be fluent in English. The French aren't the only ones who appreciate good food.'

I'm always amazed by Georges' English. I've seen him at the Ritz joking with American customers as if English was his mother tongue. This fluency has no doubt contributed to his reputation in the States. But it's not the only explanation; he has lived over there, too.

'In 1979, the University of Los Angeles invited me to give a lecture on wine,' he relates. 'I was thrilled and accepted straight-away. Later, I got cold feet at the thought of speaking for three hours in English. Raymond Oliver was the one who really per-suaded me to go. "You've got to do it," he said. "It's a great chance for you. Use my name as much as you like, if it's of any help. And above all don't forget to make them laugh. At that time, Raymond Oliver was a big name in the States,"' Lepré emphasises. 'He was a wonderfully generous man, and a fantastic boss.'

The seminar was a great success. The students were fascinated, and listened as attentively as if it was the first time they'd ever heard anything about wine. 'I just told them things which would seem very ordinary in France,' Georges says modestly.

Georges Lepré eventually yielded to the lure of California. After seventeen years at the Grand Véfour, he became manager of La Couronne, one of the smartest restaurants in Los Angeles.

'They had one of the ten best wine lists in America. It was almost as thick as a telephone directory. That's the US for you! During my time there, I tasted more top French wines than I'd ever tasted before. But I missed Paris desperately.'

In 1983, he moved back to Paris. As soon as he arrived, he heard that the Ritz was looking for a wine waiter. Within a week, he was at the head of one of the most renowned wine cellars in the world.

The Paris Ritz has its own special atmosphere. The clientele is mainly international, very 'Ritzy', and incredibly wealthy. The common meeting place (if you can use the word 'common' in connection with the Ritz) is the Winter Garden of the opulent Espadon restaurant, with its lavish Napoleon III decor. This is where Georges Lepré is to be found at lunchtime and in the evenings.

But, despite his splendid backdrop, Lepré has his feet firmly on the ground. Wine waiters are often described as ambassadors, since they are the last link in the chain between the vintner and the consumer. But Lepré warns that members of his profession should remain humble: 'After all, we don't make anything. We merely recommend something produced by others.'

But what sort of wines are drunk at the Ritz?

'Clients come here for the "production" as much as anything,' Georges says. 'The decor, the flowers, the service and, of course, the food, all help to enhance their self-esteem. They also come to drink outstanding wines. It's not the sort of place people come to discover little-known regional wines. They just don't go with the palatial atmosphere. A client might feel that to be offered an unknown wine was incongruous, like being asked to take off his tie.

'Occasionally, I do recommend less obvious choices, such as late-harvest Alsace wines, which I happen to think are quite exceptional. More often than not, however, I feel that the client is disappointed because I didn't recommend one of the top Sauternes.'

Give Georges a free hand to match wines with a specific menu, and he will come up with some surprising ideas, disclosing some of the hidden treasures in his cellar. Georges isn't just a wine enthusiast; he's also crazy about food and spends a lot of time with the head chef, Guy Legay, tasting his latest creations.

'Each table is a little world of its own. Our task is to understand straightaway what type of wine the client feels like drinking. It isn't as easy as it sounds; the client doesn't necessarily use the same "professional" vocabulary as we do to describe the taste he wants. Then, once the style of the wine has been decided on, we have to find a wine that will go with the dishes selected. And we mustn't forget the price!'

More often than not, it's a Bordeaux that suits the ideas both of the customer and the wine waiter. Georges might well recommend a Domaine de Chevalier or a Château Léoville-las-Cases, two of his favourite wines. Might he be accused of partiality – of having a sneaking preference for Bordeaux?

'For a long time I preferred Burgundies. Their fruitiness flatters the palate, and they are often quite spectacular. But I must admit that Bordeaux wines sometimes have a complexity and finesse that approaches perfection.'

While Georges is enthusiastic about the wines of some of the younger generation of Burgundian producers, he is deeply critical of those who continue to produce mediocre wines sold at ludicrously high prices.

The most expensive bottles at the Ritz are usually uncorked behind the closed doors of the luxury suites. Lavish private receptions and dinners are given here by the wealthy and the famous. The clientele on these upper floors has at least one thing in common: jet-lag. Wine waiters are on call twenty-four hours a day. Their task, however, is limited to pouring the wine – for the rich, powerful and famous have very straightforward tastes.

Pétrus comes top on the list, followed by Bordeaux – first-class growths only – in historic vintages: 1928, 1929, 1945, 1947, 1953, 1955, 1961. The very wealthy who entertain in their private salons haven't got time for anything but the best, and the staff are used to it. 'An order of six bottles of Pétrus 1953, at £1,600 a bottle, is commonplace,' says Georges. He has seen far more extravagant requests.

Some customers have their special preferences. Dustin Hoffman is apparently mad about Château Latour. 'Me too,' says Georges, who has a particular soft spot for the 1961. 'It's got everything. It's an extremely virile wine, yet it's full of tenderness. It deserves, and needs, to be, treated with care.'

It would head the list of wines that Georges Lepré would take with him to a desert island. To placate those who claim he is too much of a Bordeaux fan, he would also take the exceptional 1963 Quinta do Noval Nacional, a powerful, elegant port aged twenty-five years in bottle. Yquem would, naturally, be included – the 1947, an 'historic monument'. There would also be a *vin jaune*, an unappreciated treasure rarely ordered at the Ritz. And then of course, some of the unrivalled white Burgundies ... It's difficult to stop him once he starts thinking about his favourite wines.

Like all great wine waiters, Georges is a bit of teacher at heart. He gets pleasure from guiding his clients and helping them broaden their horizons. So it will come as no surprise that Georges Lepré was involved for a long time in organising professional tasting courses at the Académie du Vin in Paris. Now, he is an advisor at the Ministry of Education, working on a training course for wine waiters. He also chairs the jury. He has a refreshingly sceptical approach. For example, he doesn't believe in the sort of exam that proclaims the winner the 'best in the world'. 'Do you know of any other profession where someone is awarded the title of "best in the world"? Competitions are so arbitrary. It doesn't seem fair that all the praise is heaped on the winner, when the runner-up often deserves a lot of credit.

'Today, a young wine waiter must obviously know all about the wine-producing regions. He must also be able to recognise wines in blind tastings, speak at least one foreign language, and know how to manage a budget.'

The best way to understand wines, Georges believes, is to travel around the producing regions as much as possible. Nowadays, a wine waiter is welcomed everywhere he goes. Producers realise that it is he who will make or break their reputation.

Georges Lepré has always been persona grata in all the Bordeaux châteaux. Except once. The exception arose after he had taken part in a tasting in New York to compare the best of the Californian wines with those from Bordeaux. It just so happened that the Californian wines came out top. For a while, he was blacklisted for treason in the top Bordeaux châteaux. Then one day he answered back: 'It's not me who paid the Napa Valley vineyards the highest compliment. It's you, the top Bordeaux château-owners, who are out there now buying land and starting up vineyards.' The incident was closed.

Every month, in the *Revue du Vins de France*, Georges Lepré invents an entire dinner party around his favourite wines. His love of opera has some influence on his regular column. He often borrows musical terms to describe the wines, and manages to pull the whole thing off. In 1991, his skill with the pen spurred him on to write a book on the history of the wine cellar at the Ritz – a cellar created with care by the hotel's founder, César Ritz, who had himself been a wine waiter.

And what about his real home? After his extramural activities, his frequent visits to vineyards, and regular staff tastings, there's not much time left for private life.

'After my day's work, at around midnight, I look forward to dinner at home. I never dine at the Ritz, as a matter of principle.'

And what rare nectar does he uncork late at night with his wife? 'I have a glass of simple, straightforward wine from my home town. A Côtes du Brulhois.'

Claude Ricard

IF BORDEAUX had to be represented by one of its many wine-producing appellations, the Graves would probably be as good a choice as any. It's one of the oldest viticultural areas in the region. The Graves vineyard, planted on stony or gravelly (hence its name) soils, produces the region's lightest and most easily digestible wines. Unfortunately, its proximity to the town of Bordeaux, a great commercial advantage in the old days, is now responsible for the gradual disappearance of many of its châteaux. The few properties nearest Bordeaux that have resisted the urban sprawl look like country relics locked into suburbia. But it has a quirk that makes it stand out from the rest of Bordeaux. It has never been able to decide whether its red wines are better than its whites. And often the same property produces both.

Few châteaux in the Graves are as well-known as their world-famous counterparts in the communes of Pauillac, Margaux and Saint-Julien. Haut-Brion, the only Graves included in the 1855 Classification of Bordeaux Reds, is an exception. In 1953 and 1959, in fact, fifteen other châteaux from the Graves region were added to the classification. Curiously, however, the French wine drinker tends to drink Bordeaux from the Médoc and Saint-Emilion, often forgetting the very existence of wines from the Graves.

Such forgetfulness is to be regretted as some Graves are quite exceptional. When I was buying wine for the Lucien Legrand shop, I remember being particularly excited one day when I managed to obtain a few precious cases of the white Graves from the Domaine de Chevalier. In a good year, the domaine produces a maximum of 600 cases of white wine. The very first time I'd tasted this wine was in London. It was drunk with great respect. Among connoisseurs, it's considered one of the great dry whites of France.

My Parisian customers, fairly sophisticated Bordeaux enthusiasts, looked at the bottles unable to make up their minds whether to buy or not. They weren't inspired by the black-and-white label and the forty-year-old photo showing a view of the seventeen-hectare domaine surrounded by woods. All they noticed was that it was a mere Graves – not even a château – and that it was expensive. A handful of real connoisseurs, however, did snap up the few cases that were for sale.

This anonymity appeals to me, and I'm also fascinated by the history of the domaine because it owes so much to one man, Claude Ricard. Despite innumerable difficulties over the years, he has never compromised the quality of his wine, never taken the easy way out. Well before 1971, when prices of top Bordeaux doubled and even tripled overnight, Claude Ricard continued to make aristocratic wines despite meagre revenues.

With the recent explosion of property prices in Bordeaux, the domaine's co-proprietors put pressure on Claude Ricard to sell. He had no alternative but to accept their decision. But he loved his property too much to allow a buy-out by a large impersonal company. And so he managed the transition as he had run his domaine – with great care and intense personal investment. The domaine was sold to Olivier Bernard, a young Bordelais whose family own the largest distillery in the region. Olivier was already infatuated with wine. But his daily contact with Claude Ricard made him as obsessed with quality as his predecessor. The cohabitation period lasted a number of years until Claude Ricard was certain that Olivier knew and loved the property as much as he did. Only then did he leave, knowing that the domaine was in good hands.

A few summers ago, I was at a dinner party in a neighbouring château and was amused to see Madame Ricard raising her eyebrows as she caught sight of her husband's bright red braces. Such unorthodox details don't usually go down well at formal Bordeaux dinner parties. Claude responded with a carefree smile. His natural elegance and class let him get away with anything, even at rather uptight Bordeaux gatherings. With his long pianist's fingers, he lifted up the glass of La Mission Haut-Brion 1971 he had just been served, and took a few small, studious sips.

'You can spot a La Mission Haut-Brion a mile away', he said, never missing an opportunity to acknowledge the qualities of other wines. 'For some its uniqueness lies in an almost resiny taste. The 1971 is a superb vintage, and it will keep on being delicious for many more years.'

Madame Ricard, who had already forgotten about the braces, nodded in unobtrusive agreement with her husband. She's used to drinking wines at the peak of their maturity. That often means when they are very old indeed.

Claude Ricard's slim figure doesn't fit in with people's usual idea of wine producers, especially those over sixty. His fine, white hair contrasts with his glowing, healthy complexion. His youthful appearance is partly due to his regular games of tennis. When he was younger, he was almost in the professional class. He still has a formidable backhand, and continues to win infuriatingly often against partners half his age. He regards ordinary tennis as a pleasant relaxation. But talk to him about *real* tennis, and his face lights up. He used to be the French champion in this ancient sport, although he's quick to point out that it's easy to be the best when there's hardly any competition.

From an early age, Claude Ricard's real passion lay not in sporting events but in music. His mother, an excellent pianist herself, noticed that of all her children Claude was by far the most musically talented. It was at his own insistence, though, that she signed him up for piano lessons. That was the beginning of the end of Claude's childhood. When other children were out playing, Claude was practising his scales. He had already begun the uphill struggle that goes with being a perfectionist. He wanted to study at the Paris Conservatoire and to be a professional pianist. But a series of unfortunate circumstances and illnesses conspired against him, and he failed his entrance examination twice. Luckily for Domaine de Chevalier fans, his pride prevented him from sitting the exam a third time. But the piano is still an important part of his life. Whenever he has time, he likes to play Liszt, Chopin or Scott Joplin.

The wines from the Domaine de Chevalier are a reflection of Claude Ricard himself: shy at first, but ultimately very rewarding; elegant, distinguished, and devoid of any false or superfluous note. 'The Domaine de Chevalier is a wine for real connoisseurs,' Claude Ricard says, adding: 'Millionaires prefer Romanée Conti.' Just as well, perhaps!

Chevalier doesn't suffer from the media hype that surrounds the handful of top Bordeaux châteaux whose wines tend to be bought as collectors' items rather than for drinking. But wine professionals consider Chevalier one of the great Bordeaux. It's rather like the cult following some authors have. They may remain unknown for a long time to the public at large, and yet have a firm following among discerning readers. Chevalier is rarely, if ever, in the limelight, and is drunk by aesthetes – the sort of people who know that Chevalier, even in a poor vintage, will be breathtakingly good. Take the 1963 for example.

'1963 was an appalling year,' says Claude Ricard. 'Worse even than 1965. I don't think I've ever seen the grapes in such a dreadful state. They were rotting on the vines, and the rot was spreading very fast. On the first day of harvest, I called in all my grape-pickers together and told them to pick only the rotten grapes. They couldn't understand what was going on. Eighty per cent of my entire harvest was rotten, and was sold straight off in bulk to the *négociants*. When all the bad grapes had been picked, I told the pickers to bring in the few ripe grapes that were left. The 1963 vintage cost me a fortune.'

For Claude, however, the 1963 'has everything. It's a pure delight!' – and he has a particular fondness for this 'difficult child'.

'It's only right that it should bring me great pleasure,' he says.

Chevalier 1963 is considered the best Bordeaux in that vintage. At a blind tasting, an oenologist who had earlier failed to recognise the wine said that it was 'very cheeky of the Chevalier to taste so good in such a mediocre vintage'. At that same tasting, Professor Peynaud, the Bordeaux oenologist, refused to believe that a bottle of 1963 was among the samples.

Utter contempt for the laws of economics and nerves of steel are necessary for achieving such miracles. Claude Ricard still remembers with amusement Olivier Bernard's face when, during his first vintage at the domaine, he saw the ground covered with grapes that Claude Ricard had rejected.

But the domaine's grape-pickers are used to Monsieur's pernickety ways: rotten grapes, grapes preyed on by wasps, bits of dried stalks and, last but not least, leaves, are among his pet hates. The few stubborn pickers who find it hard to resist cutting bunches that are only 'almost ripe' have their temptation removed. A handsome bonus is given to those who bring in only top-quality bunches.

The quality requirements are even more stringent for the small, pampered three-hectare vineyard that produces the white wine at the Domaine de Chevalier. It's planted with seventy per cent Sauvignon and thirty per cent Sémillon grapes and produces a bone-dry wine that manages to combine a taste of honey, lime-blossom and honeysuckle. The grape-pickers comb through the rows of vines three to four times during the harvest period in order to pick each bunch at its best.

Claude Ricard firmly believes that it's more important to be out in the vineyard during the harvest than to hang around in the winery watching the vats being filled. The quality of the wine, in his view, depends on the quality of the grapes picked. He spends most of the harvest out among the pickers settling such delicate questions as whether a bunch should be picked if it's golden on one side but not quite ripe on the other. He gives the go-ahead if the tests carried out that morning show that the grape juice lacks acidity – a few green grapes will help give the wine that extra freshness. But it's a 'no' if the vintage is already light in alcohol, in which case only perfectly ripe grapes, bursting with sugar, will be used.

He is sometimes teased for overdoing the care and attention, especially when it concerns the Sauvignon grape. It's a variety that's generally difficult to get excited about, producing fairly uneventful, easy-going wines.

Claude Ricard doesn't go along with this view.

'A great deal of nonsense has been talked about this grape,' he argues. 'In fact, it's a wonderful variety, and perfectly adapted to the soil in Bordeaux. If the yield is kept low, and the grapes are picked when they are golden, they produce fine, beautifully balanced wines.'

Today, even when most top Bordeaux château-owners are happy millionaires, Ricard's grape-picking method is still considered far too extravagant by some. Back in the 1960s, when there wasn't enough money to mend the leaking roof, let alone buy new oak casks, only an eccentric could make a practice of discarding grapes that weren't perfect.

It was in 1865 that Claude Ricard's great-grandfather, a rich ship-builder, bought the Domaine de Chevalier, with its seventeen hectares and surrounding woods. Even in those days, it was unprofitable, but that didn't matter to him. He enjoyed collecting properties in the Graves, and owned Fieuzal, Malartic-Lagravière and Haut-Gardère, which in those days produced fabulous wines.

In 1948, Claude Ricard left Paris to take over the running of the property from his cousin. Claude had never lived in the country before and knew nothing about winemaking. The first thing he did when he arrived was to sign on for a course in oenology at the University of Bordeaux. The now world-renowned Professor Peynaud was his teacher.

'He had a wonderful knack of explaining the most complicated things in very simple terms,' Claude recalls. 'I enjoyed his lectures so much that I sat through his courses a number of times. The poor man, seeing me sign on again and again, used to say in despair, "Monsieur Ricard, didn't you understand *anything* the last time?"'

Peynaud's guidance and help was of great importance to Chevalier.

Claude settled down to run the domaine, but he was by no means the sole owner. His father gave him ten per cent of the harvest, but the rest of the profits had to be shared with the family. 'With Bordeaux at the price it was in those days, Claude clearly wasn't going to earn enough from this to keep his own growing family but he would never have agreed to let his father support him – nor would he even consider the thought of increasing the yield from the domaine. (The yield was kept among the lowest in Bordeaux at around 30hl/ha for the red wine and 25 to 30hl/ha for the white.) The only solution, therefore, was to get a second job. And that's just what he did for twenty years.

'In the early 1950s, my brother was manufacturing what was then a revolutionary product – the pressure cooker. He needed salesmen to push it at exhibitions of household goods. I suggested I might do it.'

There then began a strange new career for our winemaker-cum-pianist. 'It was hell at first. There was always a crowd of people around the stand listening to my sales-pitch, but no-one ever bought anything despite my excessive politeness. Then I finally worked out what was wrong. You must never give the buyer time to think. Or, worse still, to go and ask advice from his wife, mother or mother-in-law!'

Soon, all that Claude needed was a timid smile from a passer-by and in no time at all, another pressure cooker was sold. He picked up the tricks and jargon so well that he became the group's leading Parisian salesman. Work at these week-long fairs was exhausting, but it provided the Ricard family with the extra income they needed. Claude prepared for it as if for a marathon. A few days before the opening of a fair, he would go skiing so as to face the ordeal in top physical and mental form. He even took up door-to-door selling. Years later, Olivier Bernard's mother recognised him straightaway when they were discussing the purchase of the Chevalier property. In the past, he had gone into her kitchen to demonstrate the virtues of the pressure cooker!

His dual career produced some amusing situations. He still

laughs at the thought of a conversation he once had with a great restaurateur who claimed to have seen his double selling pressure cookers. Claude raised his eyebrows in astonishment and feigned surprise. 'I didn't reveal the truth. I knew that if I did, he'd think I was crazy.'

However, his daily contact with pressure cookers didn't convert him to stainless steel. Unlike most of the other top Bordeaux producers, he never bought stainless steel vats for the domaine, claiming that he didn't like things that shone too brightly.

The vats at the domaine are old-fashioned ones made of steel painted red on the outside and lined with epoxy resin. They were made with especially large openings at the top to facilitate the operation known locally as *bombage* (the more common term elsewhere is *pigeage*).

Bombage is carried out by submerging the grape skins in the grape juice with the help of a long broom-like handle, at the end of which is a round wooden disk. Few properties in Bordeaux go in for *bombage*, but it is done at the Domaine de Chevalier and gives the wine maximum colour and aroma. The domaine vinifies to produce wines for long-keeping. The fermentation is long, taking around three weeks, and is carried out at relatively high temperatures of 32° to 35°C.

The first wines that Claude ever made, in particular the 1948, 1950 and 1953, underwent a *bombage* which he readily describes as over-zealous. The wines had so much tannin that they were undrinkable for a good ten years. But taste them now, and they still have powerful lingering flavours.

Impatient wine drinkers who can't resist recent vintages should confine themselves to wines from other châteaux. For the wines from Domaine de Chevalier only reach their maturity after many years in bottle. The 1961s and 1964s, both tremendous, should be drunk now. So too should the lesser vintages of 1963 and 1965, almost masterpieces. They have the elegance, finesse and complexity I love in Bordeaux. Only great wines can soften out so well after ten or twenty years of bottle-age, with such an unrivalled wealth of aromas.

Claude Ricard delights in sharing the complex tastes of his older vintages, where flavours of resin, cigar, prunes and cedarwood intermingle. At tasting lunches, he never allows anyone else to serve the wine. He's a perfectionist, and pays attention to the slightest detail. He's also capable of setting the whole household by the ears if the glasses are warm or if a butter-knife is missing from the table.

A glass in each of his slender hands, Claude airs his wines, swirling each glass simultaneously but in a different rhythm. If he decides that the wines need to breathe a little longer, he puts them back on the table. During the few minutes needed for the wine to breathe, he sits at his piano and plays some Liszt.

Back to the wine. This is a 1964. It's got tremendous class. There's a light smokiness to it, with a touch of vanilla, figs and undergrowth.

'The 1964 harvest was a year saved from torrential rains by M. Tahon, the estate manager at the time,' says Claude. 'After inspecting the vines, I'd made up my mind to delay the harvesting for a further eight days. My manager was furious. We had a great argument and I ended up by giving in. He's even more stubborn than I am. I can still recall the last day of that harvest as if it were yesterday. It was a Wednesday. By midday, all the grapes had been picked and were in the winery. At 2 p.m., it started to rain, and it rained non-stop for three weeks.'

At the end of a meal, Claude Ricard gathers up the unfinished bottles and heads out to the winery. The leftover wine is used to top up casks where evaporation has created an ullage.

'I throw away huge quantitities of grapes during the harvest, but I can't stand wasting wine. *That's* criminal!'

Domaine de Chevalier
33850 Léognan
Tel: 56.64.75.27

Jean-Paul Gardère

*F*O R twenty-five years Jean-Paul Gardère was the director of
Château Latour, one of Bordeaux's most esteemed growths,
renowned since the end of the seventeenth century. This
Bordelais, born and bred, was the driving force behind the massive
renovation of its vineyard and winery.

Asked by intrigued Bordeaux socialites what family he was
descended from, he'd answer provocatively: 'What interests me is
ascending, not descending!' His rugby player's build, straight talk
and dry sense of humour often sent a tremor through Bordeaux
society.

In 1983, at the age of sixty-three, he left 'his' vineyard. But
instead of retiring, he put all his energy into expanding *Ulysse
Cazabonne*, his flourishing wine brokerage company, named after
his grandfather.

Unlike most of those who succeed in Bordeaux, Jean-Paul
Gardère wasn't born with a silver spoon in his mouth, but rather
with a handful of nettles to fatten the ducks in the nearby stream.
He was brought up in his native village of Cussac in the heart of
the Médoc.

His appointment to the head of Latour had nothing to do with
inherited position or influence, but everything to do with a child's
struggle in the 'land of poverty'. It was here he acquired the power
to force open the doors of Médoc's feudal society. Latour needed

a forceful character like him to take on the most virile wine in the whole of the Médoc.

The vineyard of Latour is planted on gravelly soils peculiar to the river Garonne. As Gardère explains, 'the difference between Latour and other top growths lies in the soil's high proportion of clay. Take another first growth, Lafite-Rothschild, for example. It's only a few kilometres away from Latour, yet the soil contains less clay. Lafite is a wine I'd describe as more feminine. Latour, on the other hand, is masculine and nothing can ever change that.' The 'masculinity' of Latour obviously gives him great satisfaction.

The first-class producers claim they are above comparing their wines. Needless to say, they thrive on comparisons in private. The people from Latour enjoy pointing out the feminine character of a Lafite or Margaux. They're quite ready to acknowledge the superiority of other first-class growths when the wines are still young (up to twenty years) – but only because that's their way of showing that Latour leaves all the rest behind once the wine really starts to mature.

A Latour from a great vintage should be aged for at least thirty years. Today the 1961s are still not quite ready for drinking. To taste a Latour at the height of its majesty, try a 1928 or the equally outstanding 1945 – the latter will easily keep a further thirty years or so.

When Jean-Paul Gardère was born in 1920, the sixty-eight descendants of the Marquis de Ségur, then owners of Château Latour, would never have dreamed that a child from a poor family in Cussac would one day run Latour. Jean-Paul Gardère might have aspired to follow in his father's footsteps and become a resin collector, or perhaps even a servant, but never, not even by the wildest stretch of the imagination, could anyone have foreseen that he would become the director of one of the four first-class growths. (When Gardère was a child, there were four first-class growths: Lafite, Latour, Margaux and Haut-Brion. Mouton-Rothschild only became a first-class growth in 1973.)

'On my days off I'd go to the woods with my father to collect the resin. It was used to make turpentine. There was a steady demand for it until the 1930s. Then the Americans launched a rival, cheaper product called White Spirit. My father's meagre income was halved overnight.'

Jean-Paul Gardère's childhood was dominated by the Depression. The real one. One which stopped poor families from eating fresh bread because 'it smells so good and that makes you eat twice as much'. Vivid recollections from this period include the grape harvests. They're not at all like the idyllic autumnal pictures usually painted.

'Our work used to begin at daybreak and end when it was too dark to go on. The big châteaux still gave us some proper meat broth at midday but smaller producers couldn't even afford that – the butchers refused to supply them because of all their unpaid bills. Our only pay consisted of one or two barrels of *piquette* that we'd take home at dead of night to avoid paying duty. (*Piquette* is a thin, acidic drink, lightish in alcohol, concocted by adding water to the skins and stalks of grapes that have already been pressed to make wine. It is now illegal.)

'The local policeman signalled the end of the grape harvest by beating his drum with the only arm he had left. From then on anyone was allowed to glean whatever fruit was left in the vineyards. It was mainly *grapillons*, a second sprouting of small bunches that appear late in the season and rarely ripen. "Wine" was made by cramming these bunches, together with their stalks, into a barrel, and adding sugar. The barrel was kept in the kitchen and the "wine" was drawn from it at mealtimes. As the weeks went by it gradually turned into vinegar...'

When he was eleven years old, Jean-Paul Gardère worked Thursdays, Saturdays and Sundays as an under-servant in a wealthy household. To this day he can still remember the weight of a size eleven shoe in the hands of a small boy. He also recalls without shame that he used to pick up anything he could find, from feathers to old bits of wool and rabbit skins, in order to barter them. His grandmother, who spoke the local patois but not a word of French, used to unwind old socks and use the wool again.

Gardère has seen too many slumps to believe in eternal prosperity. 'The only thing that's kept the wine market in order up till now is the recurrence of wars and late frosts – they help mop up excess stocks!' This is why he's sceptical when he sees Bordeaux châteaux being transformed into miniature versions of Versailles. 'The French are no longer the only producers of fine wines. They don't seem to realise they're dancing on a volcano.'

Gardère returned to Bordeaux in 1941, having lost a kidney and two years of his life in a German prison camp. In 1945, after a short but depressing spell of office work, he decided he had to be really free again.

A friend of his had a small wine business in Margaux, his wife's village. Gardère started out working there as the odd job man. He made wine cases by hammering planks together. He also helped out in the winery from time to time.

In 1947 he decided to try his luck and set himself up as a wine broker. His only assets were a bicycle and a lot of cheek. To start with, things weren't easy. He scoured the Médoc on his bicycle, looking for wines to sell, and then had a terrible time trying to get the main Bordeaux wine *négociants* to taste his samples. 'They used up all their energy imitating the Victorians! When I took my samples to their offices I could nevêr get to see them. Their secretaries turned up their noses and told me the gentlemen never saw anyone.'

Gardère, now a father, was just about to give up when a conversation with Paul Quié, the owner of Château Rauzan-Gassies, gave him an idea. Gardère spent most of his time in the vineyards, observed Quié, and he knew what was going on there better than any of the desk-bound *négociants*. Why not write a newsletter to keep them informed?

In May 1946 he wrote his first newsletter. It was called 'Business and Properties in the Médoc'. Gardère typed it out himself on a typewriter dating back to the First World War. The *négociants* read it with interest, and slowly but surely Gardère built up a modest reputation for himself. The 'gentlemen' finally opened their doors to him.

'In those days the Médoc was nothing like it is today. The

vineyards had suffered terribly during the war. No new planting had been carried out, the soil hadn't been fertilised for ages, and the vines hadn't been treated against diseases. These unkept vines produced only fifteen to twenty hectolitres per hectare. Owners hardly ever visited their châteaux. They were run by Bordeaux-based managers who often took care of five or six domaines at the same time. And even they didn't go to the vineyards all that often: they'd take the train to the Médoc and tour the properties they looked after once or twice a month.'

In those days an astute manager would earn enough to buy out one of 'his' properties after about thirty years of work.

In 1947, the situation changed dramatically, and prices rocketed. A barrel of Médoc was worth 100,000 (old) francs, the equivalent of a worker's salary for two years. In his newsletter that year, Jean-Paul Gardère warned that if prices continued to rise there would be 'a crisis as severe as the great Depression that hit the Médoc before the war'. Sure enough, by the end of 1947 and throughout 1948 a barrel of good Médoc sold at around 40,000 francs – less than the price fetched for ordinary wines from Southern France.

Gardère's predictions were right that time. But he's the first to admit that he sometimes overdoes the gloom. In 1963, for example, he couldn't understand why the British conglomerate Pearson spent the colossal sum of thirteen million francs (today's equivalent of £9.4 million) for a hopelessly run-down Château Latour.

'The Château seemed stuck in another century. The buildings were in a deplorable state, and so too was the estate: rows of vines had gaping holes left by uprooted plants; the *égrappage*, or separation of stalks from the grapes, was still done by hand; the cellar workers clambered dangerously up ladders carrying bins full of grapes, and emptied them into wooden vats that hadn't been maintained for a good eighty years.'

But despite the massive investment needed to get the Château in working order, Pearson didn't lose out. In 1989 it sold its fifty-three-and-a-half per cent share in Latour to Allied Lyons for a staggering £56.2 million.

The purchase of Château Latour by a British group is well

worth recounting.* We must go back to 1962, the moment when Britain's entry into the Common Market was being discussed. Château Latour was up for sale and rumour had it that the British group Pearson, headed by Lord Cowdray, was interested in buying.

The French, committed Europeans, have always been sensitive when it comes to selling off their finest viticultural properties, whether it be to the English or to the Japanese.

As soon as the Bordeaux trade heard of the threat, they were in an uproar. They even managed to persuade themselves that Britain's legendary lack of business sense would bring about a crash in the wine market.

All these fears and theories found their way to the office of the young Finance Minister at the time, Monsieur Giscard d'Estaing. He apparently sympathised with Bordeaux's point of view. Needless to say, Lord Cowdray was somewhat surprised when he heard that the sale wouldn't be allowed to go ahead. He got in touch with his friend Edward Heath, then Minister without Portfolio, in charge of negotiations on Britain's entry into the Common Market.

The French Minister of Foreign Affairs, M. Couve de Murville, when told of the decision, was stunned that such an undiplomatic move could have been made at a time when the two countries were trying to move closer together. A few days later everything was sorted out: Pearson was allowed to buy, the Bordeaux market didn't collapse – and Jean-Paul Gardère made his début.

In August 1962 he was asked by the new owners to value the Château's stock. His professionalism and straightforwardness instantly appealed to the British. To his great surprise, Lord Pollock, the chairman, asked Gardère to take over as director at the Château. He accepted, of course, but on one condition: that his old friend Henri Martin, proprietor of Château Gloria and mayor of Saint-Julien for thirty years, should be named co-director with him.

In February 1963 Lord Cowdray flew over to sign the contract. The new team was officially to take over in July, but in fact Gardère

* See article by Edward Heath in *L'Amateur de Bordeaux*, March, 1985.

slipped in quietly a few months earlier to try to assess the extent of the damage.

'The vineyard was in a pitiful state,' he recalls, 'with a large number of vines uprooted and not replaced. Entire plots of land had never even been planted. One of these, a beautiful piece of land between the Châteaux Pichon-Lalande and Haut-Batailley at the limit of Saint-Julien, had been completely abandoned. Over the years it had been rumoured that the land wasn't right for vines.

'Under our control, the vineyard was ploughed and fertilised. So too was a plot of ten hectares that had quite simply been abandoned. In all, we planted 25,000 vines.'

But the grapes from these new plantations could only be used to make the Château's second wine, Les Forts de Latour. They couldn't produce Château Latour for two reasons: firstly, young vines don't give fruit with the complexity required for a Latour; and secondly, the soil in the ten-hectare plot isn't the same as the fifty-hectare vineyard that surrounds the Château.

A great wine is the unpredictable and miraculous result of a combination of five factors: the soil and subsoil, the climate and the land's orientation towards the sun, the vines, and man.

First comes the *terroir* or soil. Jean-Paul Gardère believes in the old Médoc saying that 'to make good wine the vines must see the sea'.* In all his years at Latour, how many times must he have told people, 'The Latour vines are all within a kilometre of the river Gironde', as he pointed to the highest part of the vineyard and the three gentle slopes leading down to the river. 'It's the perfect site. The best soils in the Médoc are those nearest the river. At Latour, it's the clay, and proper drainage to avoid excess humidity, which make that special difference.'

The quality of a vintage, on the other hand, depends solely on the climate and on its annual manifestation in the form of the weather. It's in the hands of the gods, a notion that delights Jean-Paul Gardère because it puts man back in his proper humble place.

---

* This theory is questioned by Roger Dion. He explains that vineyards were planted near waterways not because the soil was exceptionally suited to vineyards, but simply because boats were the easiest way to transport wine before the railways were built.

See *Histoire de la vigne et du vin en France des origines au xixe siècle* by Roger Dion (Paris, 1959).

Two of the greatest vintages of the century arose from natural disaster. In 1945 snow fell on 1 May and was followed by a severe frost. The frost came even later for the 1961 vintage. It hit the vines on 29 May, when they were in full flower, destroying five-sixths of the potential crop.

'Imagine a bitch left with only one of her six puppies. The remaining puppy will naturally be plump and well fed. The same sort of thing happened in 1961. The vine had prepared itself to feed six times as many grapes as it actually had. So in fact it was the frost that created one of the most memorable vintages of the century! But each rule has its exceptions and 1970, 1982, 1989 and 1990 were superb yet abundant vintages.

'All four of them produced huge crops, which logically should have brought about a drop in quality. But nature outdid itself. When I was in Tokyo once, I remember comparing the 1970 Latour to Général de Gaulle: haughty, severe, proud, rigid, aloof.

'The 1982, one of the great vintages of this century, has a completely different style. Nature probably wanted to give us all a lesson in modesty, showing that our rules and forecasts are irrelevant, and all is in her hands: both quantity and quality were exceptional. The vines were given just what they needed in the way of rain and sunshine. The 1982 is a great vintage. It's lavish and voluptuous and quite unlike what we are used to seeing in the Médoc.'

After the soil and the climate come the vines themselves. The greatness of the wine depends on the quality of the grape variety, the pruning and the age of the vines. The basic rule of thumb is that the less a vine produces, the better its wine will be.

'At Latour, the average age of the vines is very great. And we don't risk changing that average by replanting a whole plot. Vines that have become too old to produce are replaced one by one. The young vines are marked and their plentiful bunches are harvested apart, to be made into Latour's second wine.'

Last but not least is the presence of man. His role runs from the pruning of the vines right through to the bottling. A wine's quality depends largely on him; he inevitably leaves his imprint on it. A number of wine tasters talk of the 'Gardère style' when referring to the perfect Latours from 1960 to 1970. Jean-Paul Gardère deals with this subject with exemplary restraint, and shifts the discussion to another ground.

'Man's role is important. There's no doubt about that. But we mustn't forget that Latour has been great for three centuries. Look at it that way, and my time at Latour is insignificant! And there's another point: one man alone can't make a great wine – it's the team work that counts. When I took over the running of Latour, Pearson told me I had two tasks. One was to make a great wine, but I was also to ensure that the workers had decent salaries and proper housing. I did my utmost to follow those directives.

'I paid special attention to those who were working in the vineyard. Traditionally they were treated like country bumpkins, even by the other employees on the domaine. But it mustn't be forgotten that they are the ones who hold the domaine's assets. Pruning is much more than just a skill. Teach someone to prune for a month and then let him loose in the vineyard. He'll cut stems for you all right, but that's not pruning. A good pruner must have a deep-rooted respect for the vine.

'Latour was one of the first châteaux to pay its vineyard workers more. It almost caused a revolution. I had to explain to those who worked in the winery that, to start with, they had the great advantage of working under a roof. Basically all that was required was that they be disciplined, clean and sober. Whereas those working in the vines had the hardship post. They had to work in the wind and the rain.' (Today, of course, this is no longer quite so true. Vineyard workers drive to the vines rather than bicycle or walk there. When it rains they take shelter in their cars.)

Once the vineyard was renovated, the next most important task was to rebuild the winery. Jean-Paul Gardère threw out all the old wooden vats and replaced them with stainless steel ones – they were easy to keep clean and permitted a better control of the fermenting wine must. It just so happened that he was the first person to dare bring in stainless steel vats to the Médoc. It was considered a heresy. At that time, other châteaux weren't rich enough to buy such expensive equipment, and wooden casks were still venerated. People said Gardère had turned Latour's cellars into a dairy. It's quite clear, when you visit the Médoc today, that the innovator's only mistake was to invest in stainless steel long before the others did.

The complete overhaul at Latour was only possible because the Pearson group was prepared to wait a good ten years before they saw any return on their massive investment. Pearson was always very supportive, even when Gardère suggested audacious economic initiatives. He felt strongly, for example, that wine was sold when it was far too young, especially considering that wine drinkers no longer have either cellars or enough patience to age their wines. To prevent them from committing what he calls a 'Latouricide', he persuaded his directors that some of the bottle ageing should be done at the Château. This policy was adopted in particular for Les Forts de Latour, the Château's second wine. It's put on the market only once it's mature. Les Forts de Latour obviously doesn't have the phenomenal concentration of a Latour. It resembles the first growth in an equally elegant but somewhat lighter form.

For a quarter of a century Gardère kept Latour at the top of its potential. He left his mark on a number of memorable vintages that will hold out until the middle of the next century.

He retired from Latour, but as with all great artists he was called back for an 'encore'. After his initial departure in 1963, a number of tasters couldn't find the concentration and severity they were used to – the hallmark of a great Latour. Gardère returned during the 1986 harvest to show how 'Latour' was made.

Having helped his successor, chosen in accordance with modern practice by a head-hunter, Jean-Paul Gardère left Latour for the last time, knowing that the *terroir* would always have the last word'.

Château Latour
33250 Pauillac
tel: 56.59.00.51

Ulysse Cazabonne
13, Qaui Jean-Fleuret
BP 85
33250 Pauillac
tel: 56.59.60.55

Jenny Bailey

WOMEN HAVE HAD a tough time edging their way into the male-dominated wine world. For centuries they were expected to wash up glasses rather than taste from them. But over the last twenty years or so they have made great headway, especially in the new wine-producing countries such as Australia and the United States.

Even France now prides itself on a handful of wine waitresses and a fair number of female oenologists. But very few women are actually cellar workers. The sheer physical nature of work in a cellar is usually enough to put them off. But there is also a strong prejudice still against women in cellars. A number of French winemakers, and not just the older ones, are still hopelessly superstitious. They won't allow women near wine that's fermenting for fear the influence of menstruation might sometimes turn it into vinegar!

But there are a few women in France who have managed to overcome both obstacles. Jenny Bailey is one of them. I first met her when she was washing up glasses at wine-tasting classes in Paris. She had taken on the job because it enabled her to sit in on the courses and taste a wide range of wines. She also met wine producers from all over France.

One winter's day in 1983 she heard that a Bordeaux château needed a cellar worker. She immediately applied for the post.

Count Charles de Guigné, the owner of a Cru Bourgeois, Château Sénéjac, interviewed her in a Paris wine bar. Jenny, then twenty-six, didn't match the usual stereotype of a beret-clad, Gauloise-smoking cellar worker. Nor was she the strapping sort of girl who might be expected to take hard physical work in her stride. She was, and is, slender, blonde, and not particularly tall. And at that stage she was far from fluent in French.

But then Charles de Guigné didn't particularly fit in with the traditional idea of a Bordeaux château-owner either. True, the aristocratic Guigné family have had ties in Bordeaux for over a century. But Charles was born and partly brought up in San Francisco, and this has given him a somewhat broader outlook on life. He saw no reason why his cellar worker shouldn't be a women, and a New Zealander at that.

He had taken over the running of the vineyard and family château in 1973. It was a place full of childhood memories: he used to spend his summer holidays there. His ambition was to put Sénéjac back on the map. So he moved back from California and followed wine courses at the University of Bordeaux. Both energy and investment were needed to get Sénéjac to start producing quality wines again. Over the years, the wine's reputation had dwindled although, to be fair, some connoisseurs still remember an admirable 1964 and a stunning 1945.

Charles de Guigné's first harvest was a particularly difficult one. Throughout France the 1974 vintage produced generally ungracious, unattractive wines. But at Sénéjac they managed to make a wine that was good enough to win a gold medal. Charles de Guigné, encouraged by the fact that the Château could produce a good wine even in a bad year, decided the domaine was worth modernising.

It was Sénéjac's cellar master – one of the old school – who told M. Guigné that he needed a cellar help. But only when Jenny arrived at Sénéjac one cold day in February 1983 did the poor cellar master fully realise that a woman was going to invade his sanctuary. He soon fell ill. He was to return only once more to the domaine, making a brief appearance during the 1983 harvest.

'I think it was the worst time in my life,' Jenny recalls. 'I'd left my work and friends in Paris, thinking naively that I was going to work closely with a cellar master and learn the art of winemaking. Things turned out very differently!'

A few weeks after her arrival Jenny was the only person left in the cellar – alone among rows of old and badly kept casks. 'The day the cellar master left I very nearly did what he'd done – packed my bags and went home. I hadn't been to New Zealand for over four years, and I suddenly felt terribly homesick.'

But she decided she wouldn't leave until every cask in the cellar had been scraped and cleaned. She set to work without stopping to wonder if she was physically capable of doing the job on her own.

'When I finished at night, often very late, I'd close the cellar door with just enough energy left to drag myself to my house just across from the Château. I'd neither the strength nor the inclination to mingle in Bordeaux society.

'Luckily there were two very close friends I could call on whenever I wanted to. One was the director of Château Rahoul, a château in the Graves where I'd once worked for a few months. And the other was Jean-Luc Vonderheyden, who is almost part of the Sénéjac "team". He gives us the benefit of his sound advice whenever we feel we need an outside opinion.'

But Jenny did accept tasting invitations whenever she could. She was keen to see how Sénéjac measured up to its neighbours. It was at one of these tastings that she met her future husband, Charles Dobson – an Englishman who, following in his grandfather's footsteps, works for a Bordeaux wine *négociant*.

By 1986 the vineyard had been completely restructured with extensive new plantations. Charles de Guigné then turned his attention to the cellars. A new winery was designed and built, complete with stainless steel casks and the latest sophisticated winepress. It's now one of the most modern wineries in the Médoc, rivalling many top *Cru Classé* wineries. According to Guigné, his single reason for embarking on such a colossal investment was so that 'Jenny might make the best possible wine'.

The new building isn't ostentatious: unlike some trendy Bordeaux wineries, it doesn't look like a mixture of a cathedral and a laboratory. Every detail has been carefully thought out, right down to the stain-resistant floor tiles which had to be brought in from Germany.

The newly installed computer that automatically controls the temperature of the stainless steel vats has changed Jenny's life. Until 1987 she never managed to get a whole night's sleep during the harvest.

'My husband used to say that being with me during harvest was like living with a mother and a new-born baby. I used to wake up every two hours during the night and go across the courtyard to the winery to check the temperature of all the fermenting vats. If the temperature rises too much, at best the wine loses its aromas through evaporation, and at worst fermentation actually stops. The only way to cool the wine down was to pump it through a coiled pipe on to which was directed a trickle of cold water from a big block of melting ice.

'Before every harvest I used to pack my own little freezer full of ice cubes. It wouldn't have helped much, but psychologically I'd feel I'd done all that I could if the ice-man failed to turn up!

'I look back on that period now as if it were the Middle Ages. Our new computer has transformed my life at Sénéjac completely. But you have to avoid falling into the trap of switching on to "automatic pilot", as some do. They make their wine according to a set recipe. But I believe that making good wine is a matter of feeling rather than pure technology. It's got to come from within you. As I see it, winemaking is all about letting nature, and therefore each different vintage, express itself to the full. And nature is not to be tamed. You can't expect to make a big fat wine in a year when the grapes don't get very ripe.'

Jenny doesn't feel particularly anxious during the winemaking period. 'Major decisions just seem to take themselves. On the odd occasion, I've taken a different view from that of our oenologist. But I've always followed my instinct, and in retrospect I think I made the right decisions. I now know the different plots within the vineyard off by heart, and the varying qualities of grapes they produce. So it's only natural that I should have a feel for the wine.'

When Jenny talks about Sénéjac it's hard to imagine she was brought up in what the French would describe as a teetotal country, where drinking in public places is forbidden under the age of twenty-one. Few of her friends ever drank wine, and it wasn't until 1979, when she came to France, that she saw her first vineyard.

But one summer, back in New Zealand, she did take on a job making wine. 'We produced every kind of wine except for wine made from grapes!' One day she was chatting with some customers who had just come back from a grape-picking holiday in Burgundy. They gave her the name and address of 'their' wine producer in Burgundy, 'who simply adores New Zealanders', in case she ever made it to Europe. Some day, she told herself, she would swap making strawberry wine for the real thing.

She took a degree in Home Science, specialising in Industrial and Experimental Foods, and got a job in that field when she graduated. But she was haunted by the thought of going to Burgundy, and finally she got out the address she'd been given and wrote to Jacques Seysses at the Domaine Dujac.

Soon afterwards she made her way to the small village of Morey-Saint-Denis in Burgundy. It was September 1979. 'The day after I arrived the harvest began and I was sent out picking. I didn't even know how to say grapes in French.'

Jenny planned to stay only for the harvest, but once it was over the Seysses family kept her on to help in the winery. She stayed with them for two years and learnt the French way of life: how to cook, how to speak French and, of course, all about wines and how to drink them. She drank memorable bottles from M. Seysses' extensive cellar. When she finally left Burgundy she knew that the only thing she wanted to do in her life was to make wine.

'My time in Burgundy was very useful. It enabled me to have a wider and perhaps more detached view of winemaking than if I'd worked only in Bordeaux.'

But some Bordelais see their way of winemaking as the only way. Once, she suggested with reason that the maceration period should be shortened for a particularly difficult harvest. The wine-maker, obviously blinded by tradition, answered curtly: 'Mademoiselle, here we are in France, and we vinify the French way.'

'The winemaking season is always frantic. Every year there's a big blank in my calendar from mid-September to mid-November. During this entire period, I never leave the domaine. No dinner parties, no shopping, no weekends. I even get someone else to drop off the wine samples at the oenologist's laboratory a few kilometres away. I go from summer to winter, missing out autumn altogether. By the end of the vintage I'm usually freezing because I haven't had a chance to get my winter clothes out.'

These few months are full of ups and downs. There's always a piece of machinery that breaks down at the crucial moment. Jenny now fixes some of the minor equipment herself, having found out the hard way that you can never count on the repairmen to come when you really need them.

'For all its alarms and excursions, this is the time when you're the closest to the wine. When the fermentation is over I always feel a sort of sadness, like the sudden realisation that your baby has grown up too quickly. But perhaps the most frustrating part of our job is knowing that in ten years you can only produce ten vintages. It doesn't seem much.'

The vineyard at Sénéjac is planted on a poor, gravelly, sandy soil which produces grapes lacking colour. To extract as much colour as possible, Jenny uses the technique of *pigeage* which she learnt in Burgundy but which is hardly ever used in Bordeaux.

When I was in Bordeaux during the 1985 vintage, I called at Sénéjac. I remember walking into the old winery and seeing Jenny with one leg in plaster, perched on top of a vat with a *pigeou* in her hand. A broken leg wasn't going to get in the way of her punching the cap and extracting all the colour she could from the grape skins.

I've rarely met anyone so quietly obstinate. The following year she sacked all the grape-pickers and hired a harvesting machine instead. At the onset of the harvest, she had taken the trouble to walk through the rows of vines with the grape-pickers, explaining that she wanted only the ripest bunches picked. By the end of the day it was quite clear that the pickers had merely cut all that came their way. Had they ignored her instructions because she was a woman? Whatever the reason, Jenny paid them for their day's work and dismissed them all. She finished the harvesting by machine. It was faster, more efficient and less surly than the grape-pickers. All she needed then was a couple of people at the receiving end to sort out the ripe bunches from the rest.

At Sénéjac there are twenty-six hectares of vines. It's a classic Médoc vineyard planted with forty-nine per cent Cabernet Sau-vignon, thirty per cent Merlot, twenty per cent Cabernet Franc, and one per cent Petit Verdot. The one per cent isn't just symbolic: it's very important to Jenny. Petit Verdot is a vine variety hardly ever planted in the Médoc any more. It ripens very late in the season, but in good years it lends the wine a perfumed, peppery, exotic note.

'Take the 1985 vintage. We had a hot, dry autumn that year, and we waited until the end of October before harvesting the Petit Verdot. We picked it at its ripest, and during the fermentation the winery was full of its wonderful aromas. It's a highly aromatic grape similar to the Syrah variety from the northern Rhône. Despite the minute percentage in the final blend, you can really taste it in ripe vintages.

'The 1985 Sénéjac is rich and velvety, soft and feminine. It will be ready to drink around 1995. The 1986 Sénéjac is quite the opposite. It's a classic Médoc, a severe wine, closed in on itself. It has the concentration and texture of a great wine and should be kept for much longer.'

Charles de Guigné is responsible for restoring Sénéjac to its former glory, but he is the first to admit that it was Jenny who made the Sénéjac white a success. Few people know about this wine: there are only about 2,000 bottles produced every year. It's said to be the only white Médoc made one hundred per cent from Sémillon grapes.

The Sénéjac white tastes in some ways like a dry version of a Sauternes. This is not surprising, as most Sauternes are made principally from the Sémillon grape. It produces a wine with a honeysuckle aroma and a full body. Jenny is particularly proud of this wine. Aged in new oak casks, the Sénéjac white has a light vanilla flavour, but there's also something puzzling about it. It's almost as if there were a touch of down-under about it. Perhaps we weren't so far off at a blind tasting when I and a few other tasters mistook it for an Australian.

But Jenny's other pride are her two sons. Before each was born she worked right up until the last minute, and was back in the winery a few days later with the new-born baby tied to her back. 'I even brought Christopher's cradle into the winery so that I could go on working while I kept an eye on him. As soon as he could move about he regarded the winery as his playpen – I just had to make it clear he wasn't allowed up the ladders or near the vats! When he got bored he would go outside and play in the Château grounds, hunting grasshoppers and popping back from time to time, when he felt like saying hello. When he was two years old, his favourite game was rolling empty barrels. I still can't work out how he managed it.'

Will the children brought up in the grounds of the Château grow up into true Bordelais? Perhaps so, if we agree with those who consider Bordeaux to be more British than French. For Christopher and his brother start off every morning with a proper English breakfast, cooked by their father as he listens to BBC Radio 4.

Chateau Sénéjac
Le Pian-en-Médoc
33290 Blanquefort
tel: 56.72.00.11

Sénéjac is distributed in the UK, among others by The Wine Society.

Eloi Dürrbach

*T*HE TABLE WAS set for lunch in the garden beside the white-washed Provençal farmhouse with its blue-green shutters. The only sounds were the grating of crickets, the babbling of a nearby spring, and the laughter of the three Provençal children – Antoine, Isoline and Ostiane. Ostiane, the youngest, is already quite at home in the winery. She often follows her father into the cool darkness and stays all morning watching him work.

Eloi Dürrbach poured me a glass of his Domaine de Trévallon 1986. Yet another vintage at Trévallon with that deep, dark, vibrant colour. The nose, which is barely beginning to open out, has a hint of blackcurrant and spices. The tannins are wonderfully velvety and the wine is so rich and dense it is quite unlike any other wine produced in France.

In 1985 Robert Parker, the well-known American wine journalist, wrote a couple of lines on Trévallon and recommended it as one of the best wines in France for the 1984 vintage. The day after Parker's newsletter appeared, Eloi's entire 1984 harvest – a vintage with a generally very bad press – had been snapped up by American importers.

After lunch we set off, accompanied by the two dogs, Duke and Malbrough, on a long walk to see his various stretches of vineyard. The countryside in this part of Provence, near the Alpilles Mountains, is rocky, wild and austere. The air is heavy with hot, dusty,

Mediterranean scents – rosemary, thyme, lavender and broom.

From the top of the steepest hill there is a wonderful view of the three valleys that gave the domaine its name. Eloi now has sixteen hectares of vines split up into fifteen different plots scattered across hills and valleys. Each plot is separated from the next by pine woods and aromatic scrublands. Eloi planned this out carefully before planting. He wanted these 'ecosystems' to be a haven for insects, birds and animals, just as his 'chemical-free' vines are a haven for butterflies.

Eloi Dürrbach extracts from this strange paradise a wine of staggering quality which importers from all over the world queue up to buy. His wines are now well-known among connoisseurs in Europe and the States. But the Domaine de Trévallon is still relatively unknown in France. The French are, on the whole, a very conservative lot when it comes to choosing wine.

Twenty years ago the Dürrbach family used to spend their summer holidays at Trévallon. In those days there was not a vine in sight. It never occurred to Eloi's parents, both sculptors, that their domaine would ever be anything but a wild expanse of uncultivated land.

Eloi's father came from Alsace, but he fell in love with the South of France and moved there permanently. He lived a Bohemian way of life near Saint-Tropez; his friends included Delaunay and Picasso. Eloi himself was born in a house that belonged to Albert Gleizes, the Cubist painter. With that kind of environment it is not surprising that Eloi ended up at art school rather than at the local viticulture classes.

He moved to Paris to study architecture at the Beaux-Arts, and stayed with his aunt on the Left Bank. She never saw him: he was out late every night. But after a few years of Parisian life Eloi suddenly felt a need for solitude. It was then that he thought of the Alpilles and the sun-scorched family house. In the summer of 1973 he took a train down to Trévallon and decided to stay.

What on earth made him think of transforming that wilderness of pine trees and scrubland into a vineyard? 'My father always used to say this soil would produce good wine. One day, quite out of the blue, I thought, "That's it, that's what I'm going to do". I hadn't researched the idea, or done anything complicated like carry out tests on the soil. I just knew that this was where I wanted to live. I obviously wasn't going to start planting wheat on such arid soil!'

Eloi did make one conscious decision however: to use the most modern methods available to help create a vineyard from nothing.

'At the beginning I seriously thought I was going to become a modern wine producer *par excellence*. But as time goes by I find I fall back more and more on traditional methods – traditions which are often forgotten nowadays. The book I take as my authority is *The Study of the French Vineyard* by Dr Guyot, published in 1868. I still keep it by my bed, and refer to it often.'

This wonderful book was written by a medical doctor whose real passion was vines. In the reign of Napoleon III he became the acknowledged authority on vine varieties and vineyards. It was he who recommended the introduction of the Cabernet Sauvignon in the South of France.

Having read the book, Eloi decided to plant sixty per cent of his vineyard with the Cabernet Sauvignon grape. He planted the remaining forty per cent with the Syrah grape – the most distinguished vine variety of the Northern Rhône.

This unconventional choice of vine varieties, compared with those stipulated for the region by the Institut National des Appellations d'Origine, created a fair amount of friction between Eloi and the INAO. When in 1985 the wines from the Baux-de-Provence were finally granted their own appellation, Eloi's wine narrowly missed being down-graded into the most ordinary wine category – *vin de table*. This is the usual punishment for those who dare to break the rules. INAO officials are extremely fussy about rules and regulations. Their time would probably be better spent checking up on excessive yields and chaptalisation.

Before Eloi could start planting on the hillsides he had to clear them of massive rocks and get down to the chalky, sandy soil. 'To begin with I used dynamite to break up the biggest rocks. Every day I tackled a new strip. We had to uproot pine trees, bushes of lavender, the lot. It didn't do my back much good!'

The great French vineyards have such an air of permanency about them that they seem to have been there for ever – they look as if they were destined by God to be planted with vines. But then history shows these *terroirs* were shaped by man often at the cost of Herculean labours.

Eloi cleared only north-facing slopes. 'In this part of France, everything seeks the shade. Vines are no exception. It's impossible to achieve finesse in a wine if the grapes get too much sun.'

To achieve finesse, you've also got to avoid over-production, which is one of the reasons why Eloi doesn't like clonal-selected vines. He has tried out some clonal-selected Syrah on a small strip of land, but they produce so much vegetation he spends all his time tying up the shoots. Sometimes he feels like uprooting the lot!

All his other vines come from cuttings taken in vineyards owned by friends. The Cabernet Sauvignons, for instance, were taken from the best vines at Château Vignelaure, eighty kilometres from the domaine. At the celebrated vineyard of Château Rayas in Châteauneuf-du-Pape, Eloi has already marked out the Syrah plants he wants to take cuttings from.

But growing grapes of great quality isn't all that's required to make a great wine. One of Eloi's very worst memories is of the 1983 vintage – a perfect example, he says, of how *not* to make wine. 'I started by harvesting the grapes far too late, when they were over-ripe, dried-out, almost raisin-like, producing very low yields at around twenty-three hectolitres per hectare. But that was just the beginning. There then followed a series of monumental mistakes. The grapes macerated in vats out-of-doors, in the full heat of the sun. The malolactic fermentation started before the alcoholic fermentation had finished – a good receipe for producing vinegar! Then the alcoholic fermentation stopped before it had finished transforming all the sugar into alcohol. At that point I was quite sure I'd have to pour all my "wine" down the drain. But then the fermentation started off again and completed its work. Eventually everything fell into place.'

Today, Eloi thinks his 1983 is probably the best wine he'll ever make. It is dark black in colour, and a deep purple on the rim. Crushed ripe plum aromas mingle with a meaty-venison nose. In the mouth the wine takes on fantastic proportions. The balance and concentration of flavours are extraordinary, and a wealth of smooth tannins give it a wonderfully velvety backbone. It will be ready to drink in about eight to ten years.

The secret of the balance and concentration of the wines from the Domaine de Trévallon lies in a few simple factors: yields that are held right down, a vinification in harmony with the raw material, and an ideal *terroir*.

'The main point about a *Grand Cru* is that it comes from a specific *terroir*. But the excessive use nowadays of chemical fertilisers stops the soil from expressing itself. I firmly believe the use of chemical fertilisers should be forbidden in *Grand Cru* vineyards.'

Needless to say, Eloi refuses to use chemical weedkillers. The only treatment he allows on his soil is a bit of sheep's manure made into a compost.

'I do everything in my power to keep the production as low as possible: even though I've planted vines which are small yielders, I still prune them severely. The soil is poor, and it's fertilised only once every four years.'

The result is that Eloi's record yield was a mere 34 hl/ha; his average is just under 30 hl/ha. This is a long way below the 60 hl/ha yield allowed by the Baux-de-Provence appellation, and is at least four times less than the production in some parts of Southern France.

Back from our walk, Eloi showed me his new winery – a converted sheepfold. From the outside it looks like an annexe to his house. The walls are whitewashed, the wood is painted a subtle blue-tinged olive-green. The new air-conditioned winery means he no longer has nightmares about having to vinify outside in the blazing sun.

The first wine produced at the domaine was the 1976. Just before the picking started Eloi realised he had absolutely nothing in which to vinify. The local sales representative for winery equipment lent them an old winepress. And in a last minute panic Floriane, Eloi's wife, was dispatched to the Beaujolais to ask her father, the owner of a large domaine there, if he could lend them a few casks.

'Although my entire harvest only amounted to fifty hectolitres I still had beginner's nerves! But everything worked out in the end.'

Unlike most young people who launch themselves into the winemaking business, Eloi never attended any oenology courses. 'There is a lot of straightforward common sense in vinification. Obviously practice helps. While I waited for my vines to grow and produce their first proper crop, I worked in other wineries. My first wine job was at the nearby Château Vignelaure. The owner happened to be a friend of my father's. Then I moved on to Beaujolais for the grape harvest. That's where I met my wife. The last job I did before I made my own wine was in the south-east of France. There the vines produced up to 200 hectolitres per hectare. The brew we vinified could hardly be called wine! That brief experience was enough to put me off high yields for life.'

Although Eloi is not a high-tech buff he recently invested a fortune in a pneumatic winepress and nine little easy-to-clean stainless steel vats. The wine spends only the first few weeks of its life in these new vats. Once the fermentation period is over it is transferred to the cellar to be aged in oak casks.

For some time the cellar was a sore point in the Dürrbach family. Every year Eloi promised to instal central heating and a new kitchen in the house, but somehow every year the money that came in was ploughed straight back into the domaine. The year when the heating was finally about to be installed, Eloi decided he had to build a cellar. The heating did eventually come but not until the following year.

'Strangely enough, most vineyards in Provence don't have cellars. This means that during the summer the wine gets far too hot. Naturally there wasn't a cellar underneath my sheepfold, so I had one dug out. And now wine producers from all around come to look at this novelty.

'The golden rule when making wine is never to be in a hurry. I rack my wine from time to time, fine it with egg whites if necessary, but never filter it. When I feel it's aged in wood long enough, it goes straight from cask to bottle. I'm very careful about the quantity of sulphur dioxide that's added prior to bottling. As I grow older I find my body tolerates it less and less: one gets almost absurdly sensitive. Even comparatively lightly sulphured wines give me a headache.'

Eloi Dürrbach's oenologist can't understand this obsession. Before each bottling he writes down the exact amount of sulphur to be added to each cask, so that he won't be blamed if the wine becomes oxidised. But he knows very well this yearly ritual is a waste of time: Eloi just does what he feels is right.

'I add minute quantities of sulphur, and so far I haven't had any problems. The way I see it is that with a healthy harvest and very concentrated grape juice, the wine can stand on its own – it doesn't need massive doses of sulphur to protect it.'

Domaine de Trévallon is a 'natural' wine, and so could be sold under an 'organic' label, but Eloi doesn't want to get involved in narrow considerations of 'ecology'. He wants his wine to be drunk by people in general: a wine, he maintains, should be judged on its taste, not by the methods used to achieve that taste.

Now that Domaine de Trévallon is well-known abroad, the French are beginning to show an interest in it. They still find it hard to understand that a great wine can be produced from an unheard-of *terroir*, and that it can cost more than sixty francs a bottle, but Eloi does absolutely nothing about promoting his wine. He's not at all interested in the commercial side of his business.

As it is, all his wine is reserved well in advance. And even though he has nothing left to sell, he still welcomes people who make an appointment to come and taste his wine. But I don't think it will be long before he adopts the system employed by his friend Gérard Chave. Eloi considers Chave, a producer in Hermitage, one of France's best winemakers. Chave gave up answering the telephone long ago, and has even installed a video camera at the entrance to his property. By the time buyers have made their way up the drive,

Chave has slipped out through the back door and gone fishing.

Eloi's energy seems increasingly to go into making his property self-sufficient. He goes into town only if he is forced to, spending all his time in his vineyard, vegetable garden and recently planted olive grove. He wants to produce a top-quality olive oil to accompany the delicious home-grown vegetables.

Having managed through sheer stubbornness to establish the reputation of an unclassical, atypical wine, this solitary figure has a few more eccentric projects up his sleeve. No doubt they too will shake up some preconceived ideas.

Eloi is often disappointed by the quality of the best French white wines. So he has decided to try his hand at producing one. He has started by planting some Viognier vines, the only variety planted in the tiny village of Condrieu, in the Northern Rhône. This is enough to set his friends from the INAO on the war path again – and to make his clients thirsty with impatience.

Eloi Dürrbach
Domaine de Trévallon
13150 Saint-Etienne-du-Gres
tel: 90.49.06.00

UK IMPORTER/DISTRIBUTOR

Yapp Brothers Plc
The Old Brewery
Mere
Wilts
tel: 0747 860423/860017

Jean-Baptiste Besse

*T*HE rue de la Montagne-Sainte-Geneviève in Paris is a steep, rather dull street, leading from the open market on the Place Maubert to the Panthéon. Like much of the Latin *quartier*, it is full of quaint-looking restaurants serving mediocre food to unsuspecting tourists.

But ever since I've known M. Besse's wine shop, tucked away at No. 48 behind its 1950s frontage, I've darted up the street with enthusiasm. Although the shop is small, it has an enchantingly chaotic atmosphere. Inside, the slightly elderly man you see shifting cases about is in fact the eighty-four-year-old Jean-Baptiste Besse.

The Japanese and their television crews discovered this Aladdin's cave many years ago. They can't get enough footage of M. Besse in his beret, holding forth in a soft, rolling Massif-Central accent. When the Japanese invited him to Tokyo, he went dressed in his usual way – wearing his beret.

But M. Besse has never sought to exploit his image, and many of the customers who call at his shop have no idea that the old man who serves them so courteously is a celebrity. He never displays the newspaper and magazine articles that praise him; they just lie in a pile in a dark corner of the shop. Neither will you ever catch him mentioning the fact that he appears in novels by Lartéguy and Matzneff, two well-known French authors.

His local customers know their own way around the shop. They bring back their empties, help themselves to a litre of *vin ordinaire*, pay with the correct change, and then linger on to gossip with M. Besse. They quite often pop back later during the day for further chats.

On one typical day, a young American, a knapsack on his back, wandered in to buy half a bottle of wine. M. Besse has a wide selection of whites, some from even the most obscure French vineyards, but he gave this tourist a choice of only two bottles: he'd guessed how much his new customer wanted to spend.

Workmen from a nearby building site came in wanting some wine, but 'only in a plastic bottle'. He greeted them with a *'Qu'est-ce qu'il y a pour votre service?'*, just as he welcomed his next customer, a politician who'd crossed Paris to buy a bottle of 1947 Mouton-Rothschild, bottled all those years ago by M. Besse in his own cellar.

Then a rather absent-minded woman came in with a basket full of food and trailing a puppy on a lead. She wanted an inexpensive bottle of rosé. The dog wagged his tail eagerly – and several bottles fell to the floor. The woman left hurriedly, apologising as she went. M. Besse went to the back of the shop to get the bucket and mop, and cleaned up the faded blue tiles once more.

It's a miracle breakages aren't more frequent in M. Besse's narrow shop. All is as precarious there as in a small boat on a rough sea. The bins lining the walls are filled with a thousand and one bottles stacked any old way. Different appellations and wines of different price brackets end up binned together. Above the bins come more bottles. Shelves bend under M. Besse's inexhaustible and varied selection of spirits. On the floor, hurriedly piled-up boxes of wine impede any attempt to reach the back of the shop.

In the centre, more shelves groan under the weight of a disorderly collection of *Cru Classés* on top of which are stacked tins of tuna, bottles of Pernod, tea-bags, packets of chewing-gum, Nescafé and orangeade.

The resemblance to an Arab souk increases as you approach the tiny counter. This is M. Besse's favourite corner. A wall of beer cans keeps out the draughts and helps create an atmosphere of intimacy. But this is also where the cash drawer is. It is always half open, and crammed full of centimes. M. Besse gives change to his customers as if he were a croupier. He fishes out the coins, then lets them fall and ring out on the counter one by one.

The apparently haphazard stacking of bottles continues down in the sixteenth-century vaulted cellars. M. Besse knows I love this place, and occasionally lets me go down there, always shouting after me: 'Take care – some of the steps are rotten!' The stairs leading down to the two-and-a-half levels underground are extremely steep and narrow, and the first three have collapsed altogether. I shudder to think of M. Besse striding over the gap as he brings up a vintage bottle.

Once down there it's as though nothing had been changed for centuries. There are bottles absolutely everywhere, stacked in M. Besse's inimitable way. Here and there some bottles have broken because of the sheer weight of the pile. A wall of bottles two metres high has a gap in it! M. Besse needed the two bottles in the middle and just pulled them out. Why the rest of the bottles don't come cascading down remains a mystery. Giant cobwebs that look as if they'd been spun over centuries stretch across the bottles, apparently holding them in place.

Most of the wines on the second and lower level were bottled by M. Besse himself. Nearly all the labels are eaten away with mould, proof at least that the humidity in the cellar is perfect for ageing wines. But it's not much help in identifying the bottles.

'I have a tactile and visual memory,' M. Besse explains. 'I never note anything down. But I know exactly where a bottle is if I put it there myself. I can remember where each bottle is, even if it's been down there for thirty years. That's why it would be a catastrophe if someone else ever tried to help me stack or sort out the bottles.'

M. Besse has no idea, though, how many bottles he has in his cellar. He claims he is like his mother, who never counted the hens in the yard but knew at once when one was missing.

'Of course, I could go down and count the bottles. But it would take a long time, and what would I do once I'd counted them? I'm hardly likely to announce that I have the largest or oldest collection of wines in Paris.'

But if M. Besse knows what vintage bottles he has in his cellar, that doesn't necessarily mean he'll sell them to you. He doesn't like parting with the older inhabitants. His main concern is that they should end up with someone who appreciates them. If for some reason he doesn't take a liking to you, or thinks you're the sort who collects labels rather than enjoys drinking wine, he'll suggest you might find what you're looking for elsewhere. But he can be very helpful to someone just beginning to appreciate wine.

M. Besse has converted some of his customers into passionate wine enthusiasts while appeasing passions of another kind. When the École Polytechnique was located across the street, love-sick students tended to treat M. Besse's shop as an annexe to the school infirmary. One of my friends, a *polytechnicien*, is still grateful to M. Besse for pulling him back from the brink of suicide the first time his heart was broken. M. Besse spent a lot of time talking him out of his desperation, then uncorked a memorable bottle of Sauternes.

I asked M. Besse if he remembered this episode. Of course he did: he even recalled the bottle of vintage Banyuls they'd drunk that evening, and the name of the girl the student eventually married. He was clearly talking about someone else. How many amorous students has he transformed into wine lovers? He hasn't a clue, just as he has no idea how many bottles there are down in his cellar.

'When I bought this place in 1932 it was a grocery shop, and wine took up only a small space. We sold everything, including fruit and vegetables. The students from across the road weren't just customers, they were friends. They used to hide their knapsacks in the back of the shop and meet their so-called *fiancées* here before setting off on forbidden weekends together. I'd often uncork a bottle of wine to show them the wonderful diversity of French wines. Take Banyuls, for example – it's always been my favourite fortified wine, although it's never been in fashion. It still doesn't get the praise it deserves. Age it in the cellar for a few years and you'll have something really special.'

M. Besse doesn't fit in with the new generation of wine specialists, those who bombard their audience with a far-fetched string of adjectives.

He prefers to uncork a bottle and let it speak for itself. Reaching for a Banyuls 1933 that he bottled himself, he demonstrates how mellow it can become with age. The sweetness has subsided, giving way to a gentle, beautifully balanced wine with a walnut tang.

People tend to drink Banyuls as an aperitif, yet it goes very well with a bizarre range of foods. The classic association, as with port, is with blue cheeses such as Stilton or Roquefort. But it can also accompany *foie gras*, is one of the few wines that stand up to a chocolate dessert, and for the more adventurous it goes curiously well with anchovies.

'On the whole I drink very little nowadays, but I always have a glass or two of Banyuls with my lunch,' says M. Besse. 'It's a natural product, it tastes delicious, and it does me good!'

M. Besse's first visit to a vineyard was in 1939, seven years after he'd bought his shop. A wine broker cum salesman invited him to Bordeaux for a short visit. In those days, professionals drank wine rather than just wet their lips with it – the professional obsession with spitting rather than swallowing wines came much later. M. Besse and his companion 'did' Yquem without spitting and then went on to taste in a few more properties. That evening they were invited to dinner at a château in Saint-Emilion.

'The owner poured me a glass of red wine and asked me what I thought it was. I knew nothing about wine in those days, but muttered something about it being a Médoc. The salesman gave me a sharp kick under the table. Later on he said, 'You idiot – Médoc is never served in Saint-Emilion, and Saint-Emilion is never served in Médoc.'

From that day, M. Besse never stated out loud, at blind tastings, where he thought the wine was from.

'When I watch top oenologists on television, I notice they too have adopted this system. They're careful to avoid taking risks.

The more adventurous ones might go as far as to suggest the village they think the wine came from, but they often get it wrong.'

Although M. Besse is naturally discreet, he's also got a strong rebellious streak to his character. I remember a tasting at Bordeaux when we sat at the same table with a number of other wine professionals and château-owners. Their heads were bowed and they were all sniffing their wine, trying to identify its aromas. M. Besse, amused by this sight, mentioned the word cinnamon. Everyone sniffed again and greeted this suggestion enthusiastically, saying 'It's so obvious – why didn't we think of it?'

On our flight back M. Besse admitted he hadn't smelt cinnamon on the wine at all – he just felt like having a bit of fun at everyone else's expense. He was obviously delighted with the outcome. His blue eyes shone with mischief, as they must have shone when he was a child in the village of Lagraulière in Corrèze, where his father had a thriving business as a miller.

M. Besse developed plenty of common sense during his Corrèze childhood, often at the expense of schoolwork. By taking a short cut through the woods he only had to walk three kilometres to school. The problem with the 'short cut' was that he found the woods far more interesting than his studies.

'I often used to poach fish in the stream instead of going to school, and sell my catch to the *patronne* of the local hotel-restaurant. I always remember my mother's advice: "Feel the weight of the fish before you sell them. That woman will swindle you if you give her half a chance."

It was at about this time that his parents gave him his first glass of great wine. He was just fourteen, but he still remembers that bottle of Bordeaux, a present from his cousin. 'It was Château Cos d'Estournel. I'll never forget the gold netting over the bottle and the name of the Château-owners – Latreille and Ginestet.'

From that moment on he became more interested in wine and food. When he was fifteen the *patronne* who bought his fish noticed he wasn't just another country bumpkin. She suggested that her brother should take him on as an apprentice in his grocer's shop in Neuilly, a smart suburb of Paris.

'I'll always remember that first day in Paris,' M. Besse recalls. 'It was the tenth of September, 1922. It's not that I was especially dazzled by Paris, but that happened to be the day of the annual fête in our village.

'My parents were sad to see me go, but my eldest brother told them I wouldn't hold out for more than a week. He was wrong. I stayed five years at the grocery, and then did my two years of military service. It was during this time that my father died.'

The children inherited his savings. Jean-Baptiste felt he should claim his share straightaway and invest it. Much to his family's surprise he bought a grocery in the rue de la Montagne-Sainte-Geneviève.

'At that stage I never thought I'd stay here all my life, but I knew it was the only way to be sure of getting hold of my share of the inheritance. I could never have bought the shop without it. Banks didn't lend as easily then as they do today.'

M. Besse remembers all the wines he bought in those days. 'It was quite simple: I bought what sold well – Bordeaux, Burgundies and wines from Algeria. The wine was delivered in casks. I bottled part of it at the back of the shop, but there were always three casks of more ordinary wine in the front of the shop for customers who came in with their own bottles.'

At the age of twenty-four M. Besse married a woman from Brittany and she was left to run the shop during the war. Her husband was away for five years. He fought on the northern and eastern fronts, was taken prisoner and escaped a number of times. At the end of the war he was decorated, and returned home with only one desire: to get back to running his shop in the *quartier Latin*.

'I've never employed a permanent assistant. Occasionally, when we really got busy, I used to take on someone to help me with deliveries, but basically I can't stand watching other people work!'

Even though M. Besse is very sociable and loved by everyone in the neighbourhood, he is fiercely independent. He never asks anyone for explanations, and doesn't give any either.

He has a soft spot for difficult and solitary characters. 'I used to like "le petit Robert". His mother threw him into the Seine when he was born in 1895, but he was saved by fishermen. I don't suppose he ever got over that. After the war he became a tramp, but he was a good fellow and helped me in the shop from time to time. I eventually got him a bedroom further up the street. When he died I went to see the parish priest and got him to celebrate a mass for him. Robert always said that's how he wanted to go.

'The last help I had stole a cardboard box in which I hid all my ten-franc pieces. The box, which originally contained a bottle of cognac, was on the shelf next to the other bottles of cognac. I noticed it had disappeared three minutes after the boy left. A pity, because he was a bright lad. Bright enough to nick the kitty!' says M. Besse, chuckling to himself.

Even though he hasn't fallen for the trend of describing aromas, he's well aware that customers don't just come to buy wine. What they really want to hear about is themselves. M. Besse enjoys playing up to that. 'If I sell a bottle of wine to a woman with too much make-up on, I tell her the winemaker knows how to improve on nature. But if I sell the same bottle to an attractive and unaffected girl, I tell her the wine is *franc*, light and perfectly natural.' He assumes all wine sellers share this *complicité*. 'You used to be a wine merchant yourself, Fiona,' he once said to me. 'You know as well as I do that our job isn't just selling wine.'

What bores M. Besse more than anything is describing a wine at length, as a well-known American wine journalist found out to his surprise. I happened to be in the shop that day and noticed M. Besse growing increasingly exasperated with the American's persistent questioning about the flavour of some of the wines. Finally M. Besse answered: 'I've tried to sell good wine on the Montagne-Sainte-Geneviève for the last fifty-six years, Monsieur, but I've never tried to sell hot air.'

'This shop entails as much being with people as with wine,' he admits happily. But the poacher in him still occasionally shows through. 'I may seem good-natured and easy to get on with, but I always keep my eyes well skinned.'

Jean-Baptiste Besse
48, rue de la Montagne-Sainte-Geneviève
75005 Paris
tel: 43.25.35.80

Bruno Clair

*B*URGUNDY should be a beginner's delight. Compared to most French wine regions, it is small and has been planted with vines along the same ridge since the third century. Drive fifty kilometres from Dijon via Beaune to Chagny, and all the famous wine villages roll by on the right-hand side. But the Burgundians have such a wonderful knack for confusing things that you sometimes wonder if they do it on purpose – even the keenest wine buffs have difficulty remembering which wine is a *Premier Cru* or a *Grand Cru*.

In Burgundy, there aren't, unlike Bordeaux, just ten important appellations and a hundred top châteaux producing one hundred great wines: there are more like 200 appellations, with 200 growers producing 40,000 different wines.

One of the main problems in Burgundy is that few producers own the kind of large monopolies that exist in Bordeaux. The division of Burgundy's vineyards into tiny plots dates back to the French Revolution when the Church, which owned most of the vineyards, had to sell its huge properties to a multitude of peasants. Fragmentation continued with the abolition of the rights of primogeniture and multiplied with inter-communal marriages, with the result that a typical Burgundian producer nowadays owns a few rows of vines in a number of different appellations.

But, an optimist might remark, surely even if a domaine's vines are scattered throughout Burgundy, the wines themselves can't taste that different from one another? There is, after all, only one vine variety for red wines (Pinot Noir) and one main one for whites (Chardonnay) and, furthermore, the vines are planted on the same ridge. What most people don't realise, however, is that the Burgundians are obsessed with the composition of their soil and subsoil. It varies not only from one village to the next, but often from one plot to the next. It is this that leads to Burgundy's extraordinarily complicated system of wine classification.

Some wine drinkers refuse to get caught up in Burgundy's bewildering maze, and simply buy their wine according to price on the basis that an expensive bottle should contain wine of quality. But to make that assumption would be totally wrong, for both good and bad *négociants* and producers may own vines in the same celebrated vineyards and use the name to charge high prices. Unless the wine drinker knows which producer or *négociant* makes quality wine, he'll probably end up like many others – sadly disappointed by his flabby, unexciting and expensive bottle of Burgundy.

Luckily, the present generation of Burgundians aim to prove that Burgundy is once again capable of producing top-quality wines. Unlike their forefathers, most of them have studied oenology and viticulture. They have also worked in other vineyards in France and abroad and when they eventually come home they return to extract the best they can from their own northern vineyards.

Bruno Clair can't understand why people find Burgundy's wine classification system complicated. To someone whose family's viticultural roots go back to the eighteenth century, the system is perfectly straightforward and easy to explain.

'Start on the widest step at the bottom of the quality ladder. All Burgundies can be sold under the generic Burgundy appellation. On the next step up come the appellation villages. Vineyards around a wine-producing village can use its name. For example, wines from the village of Vosne-Romanée are sold under the appellation "Vosne-Romanée". There are a large number of wine-producing villages that give their name to wine. They include

Chambolle-Musigny, Gevrey-Chambertin, Meursault, Nuits-Saint-Georges and Beaune.

'Up another step and you're in the company of the *Premiers Crus*. It's very easy – with this classification, all you have to remember is that the name of the *climat*, or plot of land where the grapes were picked, is added to the name of the village. For example, you have Chambolle-Musigny-les-Amoureuses and Vosne-Romanée-aux-Malconsorts. On the top step come the most prestigious vineyards, the *Grands Crus*. The name of the *climat* alone appears on the label, names such as Bonnes-Mares, Romanée-Conti and Montrachet.'

Bruno's succinct exposé makes the whole system sound wonderfully logical and deceptively simple. He assumes, of course, that all wine drinkers know the geography of Burgundy off by heart, and will therefore realise that Bonnes-Mares, for example, isn't the name of a village but the name of a *climat*.

Further, to keep things sounding logical, he skips over the various little exceptions that add to Burgundy's charm. Many villages, *Grands Crus*, for instance, borrow part or all of their name from the *Grand Cru* vineyard: thus Chambertin is a *Grand Cru* located in the village of Gevrey-Chambertin. Le Corton – the only red *Grand Cru* in the Côte de Beaune – is divided into *sub-climats* and appears accompanied by the name of this second *climat*, giving, for example, Corton-Bressandes (not, of course, to be confused with a *Premier Cru* such as Aloxe-Corton-les-Maréchaudes).

Once you've understood this, you'll have understood almost everything. But not quite everything. Because even when you've sorted out the *Premiers Crus* from the *Grands Crus*, you'll still have to learn which producer on that specific plot of land makes great wines and which sells wines unworthy of their *Grand Cru* status and price.

Bruno's family on his father's side have been wine producers since the eighteenth century. Their love of the vineyard is as strong as their love of wine. 'That's because Burgundians have peasant roots rather than aristocratic ones,' Bruno points out. 'We're very attached to the soil.' Looking at him in his well-cut corduroy suit, one would be hard-pressed to detect the peasant lineage; but watch Bruno out among the vines, and it's quite clear that he's used to working hard there every day.

Bruno often has to explain the various classifications in Burgundy to his clients, for he produces no fewer than fifteen different appellations spread over eighteen hectares. In Gevrey-Chambertin alone he has five different appellations: 2,200 square metres have the appellation villages; just over two hectares are *Premiers Crus* (Gevrey-Chambertin-Clos-Saint-Jacques, Clos-du-Fonteny and Cazetiers); and almost an entire hectare is the famous *Grand Cru* Chambertin-Clos-de-Bèze. This latter is yet another exception to the classification of Burgundies: Chambertin-Clos-de-Bèze can be sold under the name of Chambertin, but not all Chambertins have the Clos-de-Bèze appellation! (The name of the prestigious Chambertin vineyard means literally *le champ du père Bertin* – Old Bertin's field. The name Clos-de-Bèze came originally from a walled vineyard that belonged to Bèze Abbey.)

Most of Bruno's vines, a full eleven hectares, are in Marsannay, the very first wine-producing village that one comes to when travelling down from Dijon. Marsannay has always been overshadowed by its more prestigious neighbours a few kilometres further south, but it was Bruno's grandfather's adopted home.

'He was actually born fifty kilometres further south in Santenay,' Bruno explains. 'If it hadn't been for the First World War he probably would never have left his modest background and his family's few hectares of vines. But before returning to the front at Verdun his regiment was ordered to rest at Marsannay. My grandfather, Joseph Clair, then a young officer, fell in love with one of the girls of the Daü family, who owned a domaine. They were married in 1919.'

One of the first things his grandfather did was to uproot the Gamay and Bourgogne Aligoté vine varieties used to produce the cheap wines that had been much in demand in the neighbouring town of Dijon. He replaced them with the two quality vine varieties of Burgundy, the Pinot Noir and Chardonnay, which had traditionally been planted in Marsannay since the eighteenth century.

During the post-war slump, Bruno's grandfather realised he had to have an original marketing idea if he wanted to sell his wine. He was the first person in Marsannay to produce a rosé. This light, amusing Clair-Daü rosé quickly became 'the' wine to drink at the famous *Trois Faisans* restaurant in Dijon. The charismatic Joseph Clair persuaded the entire village of Marsannay to follow his example, to plant Pinot Noir and produce rosé wines. It was the only way the village could survive at a time when even the most prestigious vineyards in Burgundy were having tremendous difficulty getting rid of their wine at any price. Joseph Clair was also one of those responsible for the creation of the village cooperative, a concept hitherto unthinkable because of the Burgundian's generally uncooperative character!

The vineyard of Marsannay, saved by Bruno's grandfather, nearly disappeared half a century later, this time because of urban spread. In the 1960s the village population rose in a few years from 1,500 to 6,000 inhabitants. Property developers bought up vineyards and built cheap high-rise blocks to house workers from Dijon.

'There's only one way to stop developers from destroying our vineyard, and that's to continue improving the quality of our wine,' says Bruno. Like his grandfather before him, he thinks of his domaine as part of the village, linking its success with the general success of wines from Marsannay.

Marsannay's thirty-five producers fought many years for the right to sell their wine under the name of their village. In 1986 their efforts paid off. 'Marsannay will probably never be allowed the appellation *Grand Cru*,' Bruno says, showing an uncharacteristic detachment towards his native village. But, despite this reticence, he obviously half hopes that one day Marsannay will be declared a *Premier Cru*

'The vineyard stretches over three hills,' he explains. 'Each one has a different *terroir*, producing differently styled wines. I already print the name of the *climats* where the grapes come from on my Marsannay labels. Les Vaudenelles, for instance, gives a fruity, aromatic and supple wine. Les Longeroies (literally *longs rangs*, or long rows of vines) is located halfway down the hillside on richer soils with more clay. The wine has a fuller body and needs to be kept longer before drinking.'

The Burgundian mania for referring to the hundreds of different *climats* that sub-divide the already fragmented vineyard is quite understandable to those who live there. Each parcel of land has a slightly different soil composition, a slightly different exposure to the sun, producing a slightly different wine. The poorest soils are at the top of the ridge, but they become increasingly rich as one moves down the slope. The quality doesn't change dramatically from one row to the next, but does as one reaches the bottom. Purists refer disparagingly to the fertile soil bordering the plain as fit only to grow cabbages!

Although a poor soil is one of the prerequisites for making quality wine, the amount of sunshine in such a northern vineyard is equally important. Vineyards at the top of the ridge get an hour less sunshine every day. This has to be compensated for by delaying the picking of the grapes by a few weeks, often until October, in the hope that the weather will continue to be sunny rather than rainy. The best-placed vineyards, therefore, are those halfway down. Here the soil is still relatively poor, and the vines get a maximum number of sun hours per day.

Bruno is so attached to each of his rows of vines it seems impossible he should ever have wanted to do anything else but work in wine. When he left high school, however, he refused to follow in his father's and grandfather's footsteps. Instead, he set off with two friends to the barren plateaux of the Lozère, near the Massif Central. There they spent four solitary years as shepherds.

'We might have been living in another century. Once, we turned up at a completely isolated house where two scruffy brothers lived. They were very suspicious of us when we arrived, and they spoke in such a strong dialect we had trouble understanding them. But when they realised we'd come to shear their sheep, they disappeared into another room. They returned dressed in their Sunday best, and set about preparing a feast.' Later on Bruno found out that the shearers were the only outsiders the brothers ever saw.

Eventually, Bruno realised that being a shepherd wasn't particularly enriching or rewarding. When he sheared, it reminded him of when he was a child and his grandfather let him hold a pair of secateurs and taught him to prune a vine. Finally he decided to abandon his current stark lifestyle and return to Burgundy: the challenge he'd been looking for was perhaps simply in a row of vines as it had been for his family over generations.

Bruno returned knowing full well there was no chance of working in the family domaine itself. In any case, he wanted to start out on his own. But that is no easy feat in Burgundy, unless one's a millionaire.

When I first met Bruno he took me to see the highest vineyard in the village of Morey-Saint-Denis. It had taken him a year to clear its steep, rocky, barren soil.

'I wanted to rent some vines in a prestigious appellation, but naturally I couldn't find anything at a reasonable price. However, while I was walking through the vineyards I noticed a rocky piece of scrubland on the upper limit of Morey-Saint-Denis. I was quite surprised, because in Burgundy every square metre of precious vineyard land is already planted with vines.'

This particular patch of land, by contrast, looked as if it had never been cultivated, but this didn't put Bruno off. He got special tractors that could work on steep slopes, bulldozers and dynamite, and blasted away huge rocks to reach the thin layer of earth. (One more example of how great vineyards are often man-made.)

Bruno is particularly fond of this vineyard that he toiled to create. 'When we finally finished planting it, I was worried that the vines wouldn't survive because the soil isn't really soil but rock! A few rows of vines did in fact die, but we eventually found a graft that managed to adapt itself to these harsh conditions.

'This vineyard keeps on surprising me. It never produces what I expect it to. Some rows of vines are planted on a chalky rock bed without the slightest trace of clay. Normally they should produce lightly coloured, aromatic wines. But instead the Pinot Noir grapes here give complex, tannic wines, as if they had come from older vines planted on a richer soil. My theory is that the rock shelf is so barren that the vines immediately sent their roots down in search of nourishment. This usually takes a number of years.'

Just over half the plot is planted with Pinot Noir, the rest with Chardonnay. Bruno couldn't resist this opportunity to vinify a white wine in a more prestigious appellation than his own Marsannay. He now makes the only pure Chardonnay wine in Morey-Saint-Denis. The single other white in the village, the *Premier Cru* les Montluisants, is made from a blend of Chardonnay and Pinot Blanc.

In many ways, white wines require a gentler approach than red wines. For instance, Bruno's white wines aged in oak casks are stirred regularly. This slow swaying movement mixes up the lees, or wine yeast, that has fallen to the bottom of the cask. The theory is that by putting the lees back in suspension you nourish the wine, which then takes on richer and more expansive flavours.

Burgundian wine growers are fanatical collectors. It's always the appellation that they don't have which they dream of vinifying. If Bruno was prepared to spend a year attacking rock on a patch of land so that he could vinify a Morey-Saint-Denis, the odds were he would be ready to do it again if it would enable him to vinify an appellation he still hadn't got.

'How could I possibly resist a Chambolle-Musigny? It's perhaps my favourite wine in the whole of Burgundy. It combines the most delicate, refined and perfumed of bouquets with a wonderfully velvety texture.'

When Bruno noticed 7,500 square metres of brushwood in the middle of the appellation, he did a double-take. Without wishing to be nicknamed the obsessive land clearer, he wasn't going to let a wonderful piece of virgin land go to waste.

But before he could start blasting the rocks he had a fair amount of research to do. In Burgundy, a piece of land covering 7,500 square metres couldn't possibly belong to just one person. It turned out that this abandoned scrubland belonged to no less than twelve owners. That meant twelve different people, spread across France, to be contacted and persuaded to sell. The delicate negotiations were taken on by Bruno's brother, Michel, who has a senior

administrative job in Paris. Whenever he can get away, he goes to
Marsannay, for his grandfather instilled in him, too, a deep love
of the vineyard.

Bruno's brothers and sisters each have shares in the domaine,
but Bruno takes all the decisions. The family suffered too much
from watching the previous generation fight over who had the
right to run the domaine to enter into such battles. The end result
was that the thirty-eight-hectare domaine Clair-Daü, which had
been patiently pieced together by their grandfather, was split up
and sold.

The younger generation also understand that it's no use expect-
ing immediate returns. The general public tends to think of Burgundies as being so expensive that the happy owner of a few vines
can enjoy a lavish lifestyle. But with new plantations, low yields,
new winery equipment and new oak barrels, profits are small.

The one extravagance Bruno might reproach himself for is that
he takes care of his eleven hectares at Marsannay as if they produced
Grand Cru wines. He keeps the yields low, at around 40 hl/ha, and
the wine is aged in oak casks. At the moment his Marsannays
represent excellent value for money. But Bruno is confident that
as the appellation becomes better known, perhaps during his son's
lifetime, Marsannay will fetch more realistic prices. It's what he
calls long-term investment.

This is not the traditional picture of a Burgundian producer.
Only a few years back they were notorious for letting clients taste
an expensive quality wine from a cask and then, when it came to
selling, replacing it surreptitiously with a mediocre wine. But
customers were almost as much to blame as the producers. Swiss,
Belgians, British and Americans queued to buy bottles with prestigious labels, at any price.

Luckily, there are fewer and fewer crooked producers now.
'Burgundians who wanted an easy way of life and lots of money
have left the vineyard,' says Bruno. 'Those of my generation who
have stayed made a conscious decision to do so. They chose to
work in wine not because of parental pressure, and certainly not
for money, but because they felt passionately about it. It's a

profession that brings you as close as possible to perfection.'

This younger generation is prepared to make all sorts of sacrifices to produce an exceptional wine. Take Bruno's Savigny-les-Beaune-la-Dominode. This *Premier Cru* vineyard has eighty-four-year-old vines that produce only minute quantities of wine. If the accountant had his way, these unproductive vines would have been uprooted years ago. But Bruno is in no hurry to replace them: his wine would never be this rich and aromatic if it were produced from young vines.

The wines from Savigny, in the Côte de Beaune, are generally considered to be fairly light and easy to drink. But Bruno's La Dominode is so concentrated it can be kept a good twenty years before drinking.

'I love this wine, but the wine I feel closest to, for personal reasons, is another *Premier Cru*, the Gevrey-Chambertin-Cazetiers. Once again the soil is very poor. There's a thin layer of clay and then we're back to the bare rock again. In 1987 I barely managed to produce 250 litres out of three-quarters of a hectare; it produced a wonderfully powerful and tannic wine.'

But Bruno's most prestigious wine beyond any doubt is the Chambertin-Clos-de-Bèze. He has just under one hectare of it. At 200 to 300 francs a bottle, he reckons that this wine *should* be exceptional. 'Unfortunately, wine drinkers are sometimes disappointed because they uncork this wine too soon. They tend to forget that a Chambertin requires at least ten years of bottle-age. But patience pays off because, with age, a Chambertin reveals its splendour. The 1959 and 1961, for example, are drinking wonderfully at the moment, but the great 1978 vintage is still far too young to enjoy.'

Bruno Clair is one of the increasing number of young wine producers in Burgundy who have understood that Burgundies are no longer judged on their labels but on their quality.

Bruno Clair
5 Rue du Vieux-College
21160 Marsannay-la-Côte
tel: 80.52.28.95

U.K. IMPORTERS/DISTRIBUTORS

Heyman Brothers Ltd
130 Ebury St
London SW1W 9QQ
tel: 071–730 03324

Justerini & Brooks
61 St James's Street
London SW1
tel: 071-493 8721

Jacky Confuron

VOSNE-ROMANÉE is a charming Clochemerlesque village between Vougeot and Nuits-Saint-Georges in Burgundy's Côte de Nuits. It has some of France's most famous growths, including Romanée-Conti, Richebourg and La Tâche. Over the centuries its wines have inspired lyrical comparisons, such as 'soft as baby Jesus' velvet trousers'.

It took an Englishman to write the first unflattering comment on these wines which have been venerated since the Middle Ages. Anthony Hanson in his book *Burgundy*,* wrote that more than one grower had planted curious Pinot Noirs that produced quantity rather than quality, and that several growers in Vosne-Romanée had a heavy hand 'with the sugar-bags', meaning their wines were over-chaptalised.

Weakness, greed and a frenzied world-demand for the village's yearly production of around 60,000 cases of wine led to medium-quality wine being sold at exorbitant prices.

In June 1985 an iconoclastic issue of *Le Rouge et le Blanc*, a French wine newsletter, published an article entitled *Vosne-Romanée: a masterpiece in peril*, followed by tasting notes of the village's 1981 and 1982 vintages. Most of the wines were described as disappointing and thin. The article caused such an uproar that

---

* *Burgundy*, published by Faber and Faber, 1982.

many of us who were associated with the tasting didn't dare go anywhere near this charming village for several months. Since then, Vosne-Romanée has turned over a new leaf. Led by the enterprising younger generation of growers, it has once more started to produce quality wines.

Some growers, it must be admitted, haven't reduced their yields, because they want to avoid a dramatic drop in their turnover. Others haven't changed the way they run their vineyards or vinify their wine, simply because they were already doing their utmost to make the best wine possible.

Jacky Confuron is one of these latter producers. He's a typical Burgundian: small, round, with bright red cheeks. He inherited from his family – the oldest recorded in the graveyard in Vosne-Romanée – a capacity for unlimited physical effort. His family have been wine growers from father to son for centuries. Jacky eagerly awaited his fifteenth birthday so that he could start working full time in the vineyard. He has never stopped since.

His days begin very early. At 9 a.m. the table in the kitchen is laid for his *casse-croûte*: bread, various pâtés, *fromage de tête*, *rillettes*, a local and particularly fruity-smelling cheese called *époisses*. This ritual is sacred. Jacky has always enjoyed working hard but he enjoys eating well too.

When passed the coffee pot, he declines. 'Why should I drink coffee?' he demands. 'I don't need to be woken up – I've been at work since seven this morning.' Instead, with every meal, he drinks from a battered silver goblet his *vin ordinaire* diluted with water. His Clos-Vougeot, Echézeaux and Nuits-Saint-Georges are kept for special occasions.

His wife Bernadette works the same long hours as he does. Their eight-hectare vineyard in the Côte de Nuits doesn't allow them a moment's rest, let alone a weekend off, for they never take the easy option. Jacky is a traditionalist, and nothing will ever change him. He won't even listen to information about new time-saving chemical products. Instead of spreading weedkillers a few times a year, he regularly rakes and ploughs. Coming from a long line of wine growers, he has no illusions about nature. All he knows is that his vineyard requires hard work and plenty of it.

'My vines are very healthy. They resist disease because my father and I have always taken care of them. You can't possibly achieve better quality grapes by using chemical products year after year.'

Long ago I gave up trying to find out which is the Confurons' favourite wine. It's too cruel to make them try to choose. There are two hectares of Vosne-Romanée-les-Suchots, a wonderful vineyard on the Romanée-Saint-Vivant side, producing the kind of Burgundies I like: complex flavours with haunting, lingering aromas. But then there is also the Nuits-Saint-Georges. Although the vines there are at about the same height on the hillside as les Suchots, their Nuits-Saint-Georges is a more vigorous, fleshy, powerful wine. And then there's a minute plot of land, their most recent purchase, in Chambolle-Musigny. This gives a wine full of finesse, with the gentlest and most subtle aromas.

Despite her long working day, Bernadette always looks wonderfully healthy. This is not really surprising as she spends most of her time in the open air, tending and pruning the vines.

'In the Côte de Nuits the winemakers' wives do the pruning. It's a local tradition. As soon as you reach Beaune, the tradition disappears. There the producers' wives would rather die than be seen working outside. I get a lot of pleasure out of pruning and seeing how each vine has evolved during the year. I prune very severely. We aim at producing around 30 to 35 hectolitres per hectare in some vineyards, and 20 to 25 hectolitres per hectare from our older vines.'

Jacky Confuron seems rather reserved when you first meet him, but in fact there's nothing he likes better than a good laugh. During the harvest he entertains the grape-pickers with mischievous pranks and saucy jokes. But his natural seriousness takes over the minute he reaches his winery.

'There's only one harvest a year,' he says, 'and it deserves to be treated with respect! The winery is a man's place. Let a woman in and she'll turn it into chaos in no time at all.'

It's true that during the fermentation period Jacky embarks on efforts so strenuous they would be beyond most men. He crushes the grapes not just by plunging a stick in a vat, but the real way. The way that kills several wine growers every year.

Once the grapes are picked, they are put to ferment in large, open wooden vats. To enable his wine to pick up as much colour, texture and tannin as possible, Jacky Confuron climbs down into the vat and treads the grapes himself for three hours a day. The warm juice and the grape skins come up to his neck. 'What good could I possibly do if the wine only came up to my knees?' he asks. 'I don't get in the vat just to tiptoe on the grapes. My whole body works with the wine.' This work can be painful as well as exhausting because the bunches have sharp stems and twigs.

Pigeage, according to Confuron's method, consists of cutting the cap and then turning it over. 'Once I'm in the vat I gather up some of the cap to make large balls, which I then push down and stamp on. I have to hold my head well up while I do this to avoid breathing in the carbon dioxide that forms a layer on top of the cap.'

A wine grower who breathes in the carbon dioxide has little hope of pulling through alive. He faints, falls into the wine and drowns. But this constant danger doesn't seem to worry Jacky Confuron. 'I'm used to working in this environment. If ever I feel myself slowing down, I make sure I still have enough energy left to heave myself up and out of the vat.'

It's probably at this point that Jacky Confuron establishes his real and profound relationship with his wine. Something one risks one's life for must take on a whole new dimension.

Nowadays there are several different alternatives available for the process of *pigeage*. Apart from various types of machines, there is the compromise system whereby the winery workers stand outside the vat and cut and turn the cap over with long sticks. But even so, winery workers have been known to breathe in too much carbon dioxide and die. A well-run winery always has an extra person, a sort of 'life-guard', to watch over the workers.

When Jacky's sons aren't around he does the *pigeage* by himself. Then Bernadette, working in the kitchen, switches on the intercom and listens for her husband's regular breathing. Instead of nagging him about the risks he takes, she admires him. 'If his breathing seems to have slowed down, I walk over to the winery and chat with him. I can sense whether he's too tired or still all right.'

Jacky doesn't ever talk about the danger. He just shrugs his shoulders. 'If you're born to the trade you know what to do and what not to do. I've always done my own *pigeage*. I couldn't make a Burgundy without it. When I tread the grapes I extract everything the grapes and the stalks can give. The fashion for removing the stalks before the maceration has never given good results in Burgundy. I don't do it. But then neither do I use additives to give my wine colour, acidity, body or flavour!'

When Jacky married Bernadette Cotetidot his father gave him three hectares of vines, as he did each of his sons. In the village of Vosne, he gave Jacky some vines in les Suchots and Echézeaux; in Nuits-Saint-Georges, he handed over some very old vines. Over the years Jacky has increased the size of his vineyard either by buying outright or by *métayage*. In the 1970s, his father let him have by a crop-sharing agreement 2,300 square metres in the sacrosanct Clos Vougeot.

'In those days the Clos was split up among fifty-one proprietors. Today there are eighty!' It's not surprising that wine drinkers are rather lost when buying a bottle of this mythical wine. The quality of a Clos Vougeot varies considerably not only according to the winemaker, the yield and the method of vinifying, but also according to the location of the vines within the Clos.

The Clos Vougeot is very typical of Burgundy. This wonderful Clos belonged to the Church until the Revolution, when it was sold to a distinguished banker called Ouvrard. It was common knowledge that, as elsewhere in Burgundy, the upper part of the Clos produced better wines than the lower part. But the new owner refused to divide the Clos up, arguing that a single homogenous wine should be made from the entire vineyard, as in Bordeaux.

Over the years the vineyard did get sold and auctioned off, and eventually it was split up and further sub-divided. But most wine drinkers still think wine from the Clos Vougeot is one and the same product.

Jacky's Clos-Vougeot is firm and very concentrated. It's the natural expression of a Pinot Noir that hasn't been interfered with: an opulent, voluptuous Burgundy that because of its 'backbone' or structure is always noble, but never goes 'over the top'.

Jacky's belief that only traditional vinification can produce a concentrated Burgundy that will keep doesn't mean he turns his back on oenology. On the contrary. Over the last few years he has been advised by a Lebanese oenologist. Guy Accad is known as the 'wizard' because of his ability, according to the *Revue du Vin de France*, to create prodigies of balance and concentration while avoiding chaptalisation, and without acidifying the wine to 'prop' it up. One of his techniques goes against the current trend in Burgundy. Instead of heating the must to extract colour, Accad recommends a cool and long fermentation period.

The result can be tasted in the Vosne-Romanée-les-Suchots 1986, one of the best in the Côte de Nuits in the twelve years leading up to 1986. It is black in colour, showing that there's plenty of texture to the wine. The nose, still in its youthful phase, is floral, but it has a wealth of budding cherry and blackcurrant aromas that will keep on opening up for years to come.

Like all those who work with nature, Jacky Confuron is never in a hurry. He lets the wine evolve at its own pace. After a year or so in cask, the wine is bottled. No filtering, no pumps, no mixing. A little tap is fitted at the bottom of the cask, and the wine just flows straight into the bottle. This calm work is carried out by Bernadette. The full bottles, transferred to another part of the cellar by means of a wooden wheelbarrow, are then stacked in the old traditional way. Machines haven't been allowed down there yet. Later, when the wine has been sold, Bernadette dips the neck of each bottle in an old saucepan containing melted wax to seal the cork, and then sticks the labels on by hand.

This traditional way of making wine has attracted a new wave of producers – those who have no viticultural background but have either inherited or bought vines. They draw from this working 'museum' of traditional arts the passion and tradition of Burgundian craftsmanship that are sadly lacking elsewhere. These new producers also enjoy the good-humoured hospitality and delicious food of the Confurons' 'open house'.

Their two sons are as attached to their soil as the parents are. One has spent a year in Champagne while working for his degree in oenology. The other is training to be an agricultural engineer. But before they come back home the domaine will have to acquire more vines. A difficult task in an area where the land is already so over-divided.

Jacky Confuron-Cotetidot
10 rue de la Fontaine
21700 Vosne-Romanée
tel: 80.61.03.39

Léonard Humbrecht

FOR MANY YEARS Alsace wines suffered from an inferiority complex. The people of Alsace were much better at promoting their quaint folklore than they were at pushing their wines, which ended up in supermarkets and as the *blanc ordinaire* in cafés.

Not so long ago, nothing could have been more straightforward than buying an Alsace wine. Before kir became the rage, a glass of white wine at the corner café was invariably a Sylvaner or Gewürztraminer served in kitsch green-stemmed glasses.

When touring the neat, flowery villages of Alsace, the only question you'd ever be asked by the vintner's wife was: 'Do you prefer dry or fragrant-styled wines?' Invariably, you'd taste the whole range of wines anyway, just for the fun of drinking with the winemaker! You'd then be presented with a very reasonable bill for the twelve bottles of perfumed Gewürztraminer you'd bought for your grandmother and the Riesling destined for your next home-made *choucroute* or sauerkraut.

Today, things have changed dramatically. The first question a producer asks his customer is which *terroir* specially interests him. In order to answer that straightforward question, you need to learn a whole list of the best *terroirs* off by heart. They are Alsace's *Grands Crus*, and they all have unpronounceable Germanic names – names such as Schoenenburg de Riquewihr, Kirchberg de Ribeauvillé, Gloeckelberg de Rodern, Rangen de Thann and Fürstentum de Kientzheim, and some forty-five others.

Alsace is beginning to take on the complexity of the Burgundian system, but in an even more intricate version, because each of the *Grands Crus* can be planted with one or more of the four noble grape varieties: Riesling, Gewürztraminer, Muscat and Pinot Gris/Tokay. These varieties are planted throughout Alsace as well as the Sylvaner, Pinot Blanc and Pinot Noir grapes.

The creation of the *Grands Crus* in 1983 reflected an astonishing leap in quality. The wine amateur today has no alternative: he has to learn not only the names of the *Grands Crus*, but also the subtleties that differentiate a Riesling from Fürstentum from a Riesling grown in Schlossberg, and a Gewürztraminer from Rangen from one produced in Kitterlé. Alsace has become very complicated.

The Humbrechts have been wine growers since the seventeenth century. They are used to the trials and tribulations of the Alsace vineyard although the very first Humbrecht wine grower lived through Alsace's golden age, when its wines were drunk in all the royal courts of Europe.

But Léonard Humbrecht doesn't seem to let the ups-and-downs of Alsace weigh too heavily on his shoulders. He is a giant of a man and appears to have inherited enough strength from the Vosges Mountains to overcome the toughest ordeals, together with an unfailing optimism that is always to be seen in his smiling blue eyes.

Discreet as he is by nature, Léonard Humbrecht has an insatiable curiosity for anything to do with wine. His extreme modesty prevents him from introducing himself as the president of such and such an association, or the international specialist on the relation between vine varieties and *terroir*. Yet he is fascinated by geology and was one of the first people in Alsace to undertake extensive research on the adaptation of a vine variety to a *terroir*. In this he has been an inspiration to a younger generation of motivated Alsace winemakers.

His passion for the soil might well have begun at the age of sixteen when he started working in his small family vineyard, but the true revelation came when he went to work in Burgundy. Louis Latour's *chef de culture*, or vineyard manager, at the time, was a remarkable man, and he taught Léonard Humbrecht the prime importance of the *terroir*.

'The Alsace vineyard is different from most of the other French vineyards,' Léonard explains. 'The Médoc, for example, has already been gone through with a fine tooth-comb: the soil type is classified, every inch of subsoil has been analysed, the vine varieties have been tried and tested, and the ones that react best to the soil have been retained. But in Alsace we're only just beginning to look at the soil. We're finally becoming aware of our vineyard's quality potential.

'The vine variety has of course an important role to play in winemaking, but to create a great wine the vine must be perfectly adapted to the *terroir*. Take my vineyard, for example. On my thirty hectares of vines near Colmar I have a total of nine different soil types, ranging from granitic and volcanic soils at the top of the hills, through schistous soils down to chalky, clayey, sandy soils at the bottom. And on the top of all that I can plant from a choice of seven different vine varieties.'

Léonard Humbrecht has already handed down his ideal of perfection to his son yet he realises that it will probably take two generations to achieve a perfect harmony between his different *terroirs* and the most suitable vine varieties.

But then Léonard Humbrecht is an exception. A wine grower usually has other preoccupations when deciding on which vine varieties to plant. Take someone who has land in the plains. The clayey soil is colder down there, and it is best to plant early-budding varieties such as the Sylvaner and the Pinot Blanc. The average grower is probably most concerned about losing customers if he doesn't provide the whole range of Alsace wines. So he'll end up planting all seven vine varieties, including the Riesling, a late budder, whose grapes will fail to ripen properly leading to an acidic wine.

People who drink such Rieslings will probably get indigestion and end up cursing the over-chaptalised, over-sulphured wines from Alsace, swearing never to try them again.

If you want to win over those who have long since given up on Alsace wines, give them a bottle of Léonard Humbrecht's Gewürztraminer from the Hengst, a steep south/south-east-facing vineyard not far from his house. Memories of wines smelling of cheap talcum powder and cloying in the mouth will vanish when the green-gold liquid is poured. The Hengst aromas are closer to orange peel, exotic fruit and spices. The wine is completely dry on the mouth, with flavours reminiscent of exotic fruit rather than the toiletry counter! A few drops are all that's needed to taste the wonderful contrasting sensations of fruit and acidity. These are to wine what the association of sweet and sour is to cooking.

At the beginning of the 1960s, Léonard Humbrecht was already being referred to as a *terroir* fanatic. Whenever someone wanted to get rid of some steep, overgrown, unworkable land they contacted the only person likely to be interested.

Ginette, his attractive, energetic wife, understood her husband's inability to resist buying these abandoned plots, but she also realised she would have to manage the financial side of the business. She never held him back from buying what he wanted, but neither did she always let him know her real financial worries.

'When we first started buying,' Ginette recalls, 'hillside land was very cheap. Once again in the history of Alsace, vintners had taken the easy option and planted their vineyards in the plain. Today, growers are moving back up to the hillsides, realising that quality wines can only come from there. But meanwhile the price of land on the hills has increased at least twentyfold.'

Léonard Humbrecht bought five hectares of more or less abandoned land, the Clos Saint-Urbain on the Rangen hills at Thann. When he bought this isolated plot, the southernmost vineyard in Alsace, no-one wanted it despite its history – it was already famous in Montaigne's day.* 'Perhaps no-one wanted it because of its

* In 1584 Montaigne, accompanied by some people from Bordeaux, went into ecstasies over the vineyard at Thann. He wrote in his diary: 'Came across a beautiful wide plain flanked on the left by a hill covered with the finest and most beautifully cultivated vineyards, so extensive that the Gascons said they'd never seen anything like it.' (*Vins, Vignes et Vignerons, Histoire du Vignoble Français*, by Marcel Lachiver, published by Fayard, 1988.)

sixty-eight-degree slope, the steepest in Alsace,' Léonard says. 'But that's precisely why I wanted it!'

The soil here, made up mainly of volcanic rocks, is unique in Alsace. As the vineyard is south-facing, there is no way it can produce anything but an exceptional wine. 'I had in fact done some research, and discovered that between the thirteenth and seventeenth centuries the wines from the Clos Saint-Urbain were drunk at the greatest courts in Europe.'

Léonard Humbrecht has only recently finished planting the last hectare of Riesling and Tokay in the Clos. He selected the vine varieties by listening to his elders' advice. 'We should listen to them more often. They are the only ones left with the memory of a *terroir*. They were born with a sense of observation and a great capacity for patience, virtues we no longer possess.'

Olivier, Léonard Humbrecht's son, wrote his thesis on the Clos Saint Urbain's unique *terroir*. His studies confirmed that the choice of late-budding vine varieties was a wise one. The river Thur, flowing at the foot of the vineyard, creates a special micro-climate which favours the ripening of the grapes and the development of *Botrytis Cinerea*. The Clos is ideal for obtaining the optimal maturity of the grape. Sugar levels continue to rise late into the season, right through October and into November.

'We have Noble Rot here every year, even in cold wet vintages such as 1984. It was just about the only vineyard in Alsace to have any Noble Rot that year.'

The picking for the *Vendanges Tardives* and *Sélection de Grains Nobles* wines takes place late in the season and sometimes continues through until mid-November. As with the great Sauternes, the harvest takes place in successive waves: only those parts of bunches or individual grapes attacked by the Noble Rot are picked. The Noble Rot doesn't necessarily develop for every vintage, but each year producers in the Sauternes, the Loire and Alsace pray that it will, and so enable them to vinify unctuous, sweet wines.

Léonard Humbrecht is used to these exceptional wines. In 1986, for instance, his Domaine alone harvested ten per cent of all the

Sélection de Grains Nobles produced in Alsace, and nine per cent of all the *Vendanges Tardives*. These wines had an alcohol content of 15 to 25 per cent! Léonard, who admits to preferring dry wines himself, often has to give in when confronted with such astonishingly concentrated grape juice. These monumental wines, a true reflection of the magician who vinified them, will easily last half a century or more.

On Sunday mornings, Léonard has time to daydream as he walks alone through the rows of vines in the Clos Saint-Urbain. He looks forward all week to this peaceful interlude.

'I must admit I have a weakness for this vineyard. It's like with a child – the schoolboy who gets good marks despite hardly ever opening a book doesn't deserve much credit but the one who gets there in the end through sheer perseverance should be encouraged and congratulated. Here the vines have a tough time surviving because the soil is so poor.'

The yields in this Clos are low at around 30hl/ha. The wine is unique partly because the taste of the *terroir* comes through so strongly. Mineral flavours and smoky aromas blend in with the fruity tastes. Give the wine ten years in bottle and it will open out in a spectacular way.

Léonard Humbrecht is one of those committed vintners whose vocation came late. At the age of twenty he was all set to go to Nigeria to plant rice. 'My parents' vineyard wasn't big enough for the whole family to live off, so I decided to cut my ties completely and choose a different career. I sat a number of exams in Paris to teach agriculture in Africa. But just before leaving France I went back to my village to say goodbye. It was then that I met Mademoiselle Zind, my wife to be!'

M. Zind was quite firm. No daughter of his was going to disappear to Africa. He persuaded Léonard Humbrecht to swap five years in Nigeria for four hectares of vines. Léonard Humbrecht never made it to Nigeria.

'I spent a year at Geisenheim, one of the best schools of oenology in Germany. I emerged with completely different views on wine-making from those held by my father and father-in-law. I was convinced that the vines themselves were of secondary importance. Grapes were certainly needed to make wine, but the science of oenology would do the rest.'

After a few years of using the technological approach, Léonard realised his own wines didn't have the complexity of those vinified by his father-in-law. It was then that he backtracked and started to cosset his vines. He replaced vines that had been trained fashionably high with ones that he trained closer to the soil – a simple way of allowing the vines to take advantage by night of the heat stored up by the earth during the day.

'A vine needs a lot of care and attention. It has to be watched closely. You have to learn to adapt pruning and other treatments to its own special character. I employ mainly women to prune. They're much more caring than men – almost maternal. Their work has a direct effect on the quality of the wine and every year I send them off on a refresher course to improve their pruning technique.'

And to think that some proprietors allow only men to prune, claiming that women chat too much and aren't so efficient!

Like many wine growers, Léonard Humbrecht spends much of his free time explaining and sharing his passion. Not a week goes by without his welcoming a visiting wine grower from Burgundy, Australia, America – or even Alsace – who has come to hear about the subtle harmonies that exist between a *terroir* and a vine variety.

Léonard used to be a distinguished saxophonist, and he likes his wines to possess the same perfection as he finds in the solos of Charlie Parker. He rediscovers the same tempos in the stunning combinations of the Tokay from the slopes of the Rangen, in which scents of roses mingle with smoky volcanic soils, elegant yet incredibly powerful.

When you've tasted such wonders, it's really no longer possible to associate wine from Alsace with mounds of sauerkraut. André Soltner, a friend of Léonard's, is the owner and chef of the famous *Lutèce* restaurant in New York, and has recently been introducing Americans to wines from his native Alsace, conjuring up dishes that reveal the wine's subtlety. But his favourite meal remains *foie gras* served with a glass of Tokay from the Clos Saint-Urbain.

Although there's no place Léonard Humbrecht likes better than his own vineyard, he does manage to leave it from time to time. When he travels, he always fits in a few vineyards somewhere along the line. Those of Spain, Australia, California and New York no longer hold any secrets for him.

But he's never away at harvest time. Grape-picking is a complicated affair at the domaine. Ginette Humbrecht accompanies the grape-pickers up to the highest and steepest vineyards. She's there to avoid confusion not only over different vine varieties, but also to point out the borders between different *lieux-dits*. Not an easy job in a patchwork that includes twenty-five different plots of land and seven vine varieties.

Léonard Humbrecht waits back at the winery for the grapes to be brought in. He's ready to vinify the grapes from each different plot of land separately, as well as each vine variety. It's strange to see such an imposing figure, with such large hands, dealing so delicately with the grapes.

'The older I get the more care I take of my grapes. I no longer even put them through the *fouloir*' (a machine that bursts the grape skins to release the juice).' Watch what happens to an apple that falls on the ground. It bruises and if you bite the brown bit it tastes bitter. That shows that the slightest bump damages a fruit. Putting grapes through a *fouloir* is a kind of assault.'

Grape-harvesting machines are of course banished at the domaine. 'How can you possibly have lovely healthy grapes if you bash them across the head?' asks Léonard. 'Our grapes are hand-picked and brought with care to the winery, to be gently squeezed by the pneumatic press.'

In Alsace the majority of producers and cooperatives centrifuge the grape juice before allowing the fermentation to begin. They do this to rid the juice of any impurities, and so start the vinification with a clean juice. Léonard Humbrecht used this process for a while, but the grape juice came out beaten up and devoid of character. 'I'm beginning to take the same attitude in the winery as in the vineyard. Slowly but surely I'm becoming a conservative!'

Léonard Humbrecht's real pleasure is to taste his wine from the cask. 'Whatever anybody says, wine never completely recovers from being filtered. No matter how lightly you filter it, the wine suffers. But there's no alternative: wine buyers insist on white wines being crystal clear. I do have one eccentric buyer who orders unfiltered wine. He has even persuaded his Californian clientele of its superiority! But unfortunately he's the only buyer I know who imposes his own unconventional taste and gets away with it.'

As president of the Association of *Grands Crus* Producers, Léonard Humbrecht recently managed to surprise his colleagues once more, accustomed though they are to his flights of fancy. During his regular trips to Burgundy, he has always thought that the Chardonnay grape, which is similar to the Pinot Gris, might produce a great wine in Alsace. The only problem was that the right *terroir* had to be found for it.

He searched until he found the soil he wanted and bought it. Part of the Clos Windsbuhl, between Hunawirh and Riquewihr, will now be 'sacrificed' to his experiment. But as the Chardonnay grape is not allowed in Alsace by the INAO, the wine produced will have to be sold as 'table wine'.

It looks as though the Alsace adventure has only just begun.

Léonard Humbrecht
Domaine Zind-Humbrecht
Wintzenheim
68000 Colmar
tel: 89.27.02.05

Anthony Bryne Fine Wines
88 High Street
Ramsey
Cambs PE17 1BS
tel: 0487 814555

Michel Bettane

*T*HE GREY EMINENCE of the French vineyard is mad about opera. He is also a brilliant classics master and teaches full-time at a school near Versailles. Wine is his hobby. He fits in this extra-mural activity outside school hours, and is little known beyond the closed circle of wine fanatics. But those who appreciate wine impatiently await the latest issue of the *Revue du Vin de France*, with Michel Bettane's reports on what is happening in the vineyards and on the vintage wines he has drunk in the last month.

An intellectual in his late thirties, with the shrewd look of a medieval monk, he is sought after by wine producers throughout France. They hope that one day he'll write about their wine. But many producers aren't just interested in him in the hope that he'll award their wine three stars. To many, Michel has become a friend whose impartial advice is very much valued.

Sometimes he finds himself taking on the role of a doctor, boosting the morale of a producer who has lost confidence in one of his *cuvées*, and helping him find a solution to set it right again. On other occasions he acts as a mediator, trying to save a vineyard from being taken over by corporate investors. He always manages in the end to find someone rich enough to buy the vineyard and also – just as important – someone who is passionate about wine. He is ready to pull out all the stops to prevent yet another small vineyard from being swallowed up by a big château, no matter how prestigious. And all this just so that an appellation may go on offering wines with a wide range of expressions instead of being replaced by a monopoly. Sometimes he brings together a couple of well-known producers from neighbouring communes who have hitherto ignored one another.

At home the telephone never stops ringing. Michel's help-line is open twenty-four hours a day. He answers most queries straight off, without having to look anything up: the address of one of the few nurserymen who doesn't sell clonal-selected vines; the name of a reliable cooper. But it's not just producers who call him up. Wine merchants and three-star restaurateurs also ring up for friendly advice on purchases before printing their lists. Oenological associations invite him to preside over tastings, and the papers he writes for – *La Revue du Vin de France* and *Le Rouge et le Blanc* – often call in a last-minute panic to request an article. Despite such a full schedule, Michel remains disarmingly generous with his time, advice and concern.

When I first started visiting vineyards, Michel Bettane was still unknown in the wine trade. I remember him taking his time in each domaine, leaning against a cask and asking the unfortunate overworked wine producer the thousand and one questions he considered of vital importance. His victims would shift from one foot to the other with obvious impatience. But finally the persistent young man's desire to learn was so great that the producers always ended up by uncorking bottle after bottle and revealing their methods of vinification.

Without realising it, the producers who gave so much of their precious time to Michel were contributing to the education of the most learned and the most outspoken wine critic of his generation.

Nothing predestined Michel to become a specialist in French wines. He was born in Maryland and lived in Washington DC, where his father was Military Attaché. But he remembers as a child on holiday in France, spending hours deciphering labels in the wine cellar beneath his uncle's restaurant some miles outside Paris. One day a label was to decide his future: Meursault des

Comtes Lafon. The label was dull in appearance, with none of the usual adornments. It was quite unlike the illustrations of châteaux he normally came across in his uncle's cellar. But the unusual reference on the label to the plural – the Counts Lafon – endowed the bottle with an indefinable allure.

'The very first vineyard I visited, in 1973, was in Burgundy. Because of my childhood memories I couldn't resist making an appointment with Comte Lafon. I knew by then that he was reputed to be one of the best producers in Burgundy. When I reached the domaine, a round jovial man opened the gate, and instead of introducing himself he offered me a cigarette. He was René Lafon, an exceptional wine grower by profession and a papal count.'

Michel Bettane wrote of Lafon's Meursault-Perrières: 'It's without doubt one of France's greatest white wines. Sublime, admirably vinified, with a taste of vanilla due to its fermentation in new oak casks. A nutty, round wine that gives intense pleasure. A royal explosion of tastes, a veritable firework display!'

The first wine he remembers tasting, when he was seventeen, was a marvellous bottle of Haut-Brion 1962. When he was twenty, his friends were a jovial lot who like most Frenchmen loved good food and liked to think they knew all about wine.

'It was in the early 1970s, when the economic crisis had forced wine prices down. We used to buy great wines for absolutely nothing. But famous labels often disguised undrinkable brews. Buying prestigious wines was like playing Russian roulette. I remember a bottle of Musigny 1949 from the Domaine de Vogüé. It was a perfect example of Burgundy, and I rushed out to buy another bottle. There was one from the same appellation and the same vintage, but bottled by a *négociant*. I bought it, but the wine was disgusting. I was so exasperated by the legends that grow up around prestigious growths that I decided to find out what really went on behind the scenes.'

He read everything that was published on wine, and in particular the earlier special wine issues by Gault et Millau. 'It was the first time in France that lesser-known vineyards were written about.'

In 1977 Michel signed up at L'Académie du Vin, the Paris wine-tasting school. After a couple of months as a student he graduated to becoming a teacher. For over twelve years, one evening a week, he explained to Japanese, Swedes, Americans, French and English that wine was first and foremost the product of a refined civilisation. His admiring students learnt to distinguish 'nose wines', perfectly vinified but utterly boring wines where the flavour of the grapes alone comes through, from wonderfully classic '*terroir*' wines, which give expression to all the complexity of a soil and a vintage.

Sometimes, to prove his point, he would let his disciples taste a mature Alsace *Grand Cru* vinified by his friend Léonard Humbrecht, 'a giant who makes giant wines'.

Michel's memory for anything to do with wine is extraordinary: 'If only I could have remembered the Greek classics as easily, I wouldn't have had to sweat so much over my degree!' he laughs. He never needs to take notes.

Once, when a Chablis producer came up from his cellar nursing one of the last bottles of an old vintage he wanted Michel to taste, Michel told him not to uncork it. 'Keep your bottle of 1959. It's so rare nowadays. I remember it perfectly anyway – you kindly let me taste it here three years ago.'

The centre of attention always shifts when he sits down at a wine auction, and his muttered comments to his neighbours soon draw in those in the nearby rows. While other buyers feverishly flick through catalogues, price lists and reference books, Michel Bettane, his arms folded, merely consults his memories.

The Auctioneer: 'Pommard 1933.'

Michel Bettane: 'Of no interest. Now if he'd said 1934, I'd buy.'

'Echézeaux 1963.'

'Don't touch it, it was a terrible year all round!'

'Lafaurie-Peyraguey 1925.'

'Not a particularly good vintage.'

'Margaux 1949.'

'Perhaps, but it lacks finesse and has a slightly "burnt" taste to it because of the hot weather. In any case it's too expensive!'

'Haut-Brion 1934.'

'Ah, now that's a splendid wine! Better than Latour in the same vintage.'

'Poujeaux 1929.'

'1929, like 1982, was a year when the grapes got unusually ripe. This wine's elegance comes from the soil and the very healthy grapes. You need to taste a 1929 to know what the 1982 will be like in forty years' time.'

And so on for two half days, without looking at a note, without a mistake! But Michel Bettane's spectacular talent is no gimmick. It is the result of perfect mastery.

In recent years, Michel Bettane's profound understanding of viticultural problems and his passion for great wines have made him a leading figure in the battle against clonal-selected vines – a battle abandoned by many because of its complexity.

In a worthy effort to improve the quality of species, agricultural engineers and nurserymen have gradually selected, over the years and from each vine variety, champion vines that can now be reproduced to infinity. But Michel Bettane was concerned lest the end result should be a standardised product in which each wine's special characteristics were levelled out.

Before writing anything on the subject, so technically complicated and of such great critical importance, he researched it for four years. By then he was ready to fight off any attacks by specialists in the field. And there were several of them. 'Thank God for Bettane,' a Burgundian producer said to me one day. The Burgundian, like thousands of others, had been talked into planting clonal-selected vines. 'Bettane set off the alarm bell just in time.'

Michel Bettane isn't opposed to clonal selection as such. He is the first to admit that it has improved the general health of vines that were degenerating. But, by only keeping two or three individual types per variety, it has also horribly simplified the species, whereas the mysterious character of a great wine derives from the perfect blending of grapes which taken individually may possess defects as well as virtues. 'We can't let laboratories decide that a population has to be perfect, even if we're only talking about the genetics of wine!'

Of all the French vineyards, Burgundy is his favourite. 'Ah, here's "my" Corton,' he says with affection as we drive past the vineyard that everyone adores. He never goes to Burgundy without making a detour to see this plot of land next to Les Languettes, bordered at the top by woodlands. 'A magnificent wine, so self-assured.'

'Burgundians have a heavy cross to bear,' he says in deadly earnest. 'Their region has the most extraordinary *terroir* in the world. Soil, climate and vine variety combine to give a power, finesse and depth unobtainable anywhere else in the world. But unfortunately the wines aren't always what they should be.'

He has often raged against over-chaptalised Burgundies with no finesse or flavour. His public outbursts have often made him enemies. But such feelings are short-lived, for Michel is the best spokesman for Burgundy's new generation of producers and *négociants*. Passionate about Burgundy and Burgundians, he encourages all of them who are striving to produce quality wines. The first thing they must do, he believes, is to reduce yields.

'In general, in the Côte d'Or, the yield for a top-quality wine shouldn't exceed 25 to 30 hectolitres per hectare. For the great white Burgundies, the limit is a little higher at 35 to 45 hectolitres per hectare. Needless to say, the grapes must be hand and not machine picked!'

He is a wonderful ambassador for his protégés when he's got a glass in his hand. If he can no longer pour his friends a glass of Corton-Charlemagne 1928 – 'magnificent, but today a collector's item' – he will treat them to a 1938 Clos des Mouches – 'a little past its best, but full of charm' – just to show that a Burgundy can keep for fifty years. With lobster he serves not the traditional Bâtard-Montrachet (*Sur le homard, du Bâtard, toujours du Bâtard*), but rather a Corton-Charlemagne 1947. 'If you've never tasted it, you'll never know what a great Corton is.'

He wouldn't dream of producing the great meals that he does without serving equally exceptional wines. 'A good cellar starts with a minimum of a thousand bottles. Mine must have seven to eight thousand, going as far back to the 1870 vintage. But I'm really only a small collector. A serious cellar contains at least twenty thousand bottles.'

Michel's cellar is in an old chalk quarry, where the temperature is constant at 10° to 12°C. It's a priceless collection, though no good to burglars. There's no order in the binning, and none of the bottles have labels, which means they have no commercial value on the open market.

His collection enables him to devote himself to his two favourite sports: tasting old vintages from different regions, and preparing a dinner for connoisseurs. The results of his tastings appear every month in the *Revue du Vin de France*, and are followed like oracles by his faithful readers. 'In the 1966 vintage, Latour is way ahead of the other Pauillacs. Its concentration and the quality of its tannins are superior to Mouton, which is too dry, and Lafite, which is too thin ...'

As for his gargantuan dinners, he applies three strict rules during the service of a dozen or so wines. The first is that the aperitif wine is always a champagne, and always from an older vintage.

'The legend that champagnes don't age is a myth invented by the big champagne houses to keep their stocks moving. A good champagne is basically a wine to which bubbles have been added. There's absolutely nothing to stop it from ageing gracefully, unless the wine itself wasn't much good to start with.'

He admits a weakness for the *Grands Crus* vinified by small producers, and a second weakness for Bollinger's RD. (*Récemment dégorgée*, or recently disgorged, is an expression Bollinger has trademarked. It means that the champagne has aged in bottle on its lees for seven to eight years in Bollinger's cellars. It is then disgorged – the lees are removed – and the wine is sold.)

'I always leave my RD in the cellar for a further five to six years. I believe that's when it's at its best, making it one of the most beautiful aperitif wines, with a full, generous nose of grilled hazel-nuts and incomparable finesse and elegance in the mouth.'

Michel's second rule is always to serve two wines from Alsace 'because they're so delicious and the French don't drink enough of them'. A Muscat *Grand Cru* Kirchberg 1985 by André Kientzler, for example. 'The Kirchberg is the perfect *terroir* for the Muscat, showing the grape is capable of great finesse.'

No rules govern the choice of wine for the main course. According to the dish and to Michel's curiosity, he may uncork a Margaux 1945, a Léoville-Las-Cases 1966 or a Calon-Ségur 1959. The final rule is that with cheese you always serve a Northern Côtes-du-Rhône, and on grand occasions a Côte-Rôtie La Landonne or a La Mouline by Marcel Guigal.

'Guigal is probably the greatest winemaker apart from Léonard Humbrecht. On his finest vineyards he makes wines that equal the best in France. Sometimes I think they surpass them! Marcel Guigal has carried his passion to its absolute limits. He's managed to extract the quintessence from his *terroir*. No-one in Burgundy rivals him yet.'

So much practice, coupled with his phenomenal memory, has made Michel Bettane a taster who is difficult to trip up. One day, in a property in Chambolle-Musigny, after the wine of the year had been tasted the owner fetched an old bottle for Michel to taste blind. I realised that he was trying to catch our friend out.

But Michel recognised the vintage straight off. The colour of well-stewed Orange Pekoe tea meant to him that it was a 1953. It was obvious the wine came from the domaine, so all Michel had to do was remember the different plots that made up the property when his grandfather was alive. A cinch. But after he had conjured up the domaine's different *climats*, he hesitated between a Chambolle-Musigny and a Chambertin. The owner was astonished at Michel's accuracy: the wine was a Chambertin-Musigny. In 1953 the grandfather didn't have enough grapes to make a full cask of Chambertin, so he decided to blend the Chambertin with the Chambolle-Musigny. He sold it as Musigny when a customer asked for a 'feminine' wine, or as Chambertin if a muscular wine was required.

To avoid becoming too Frenchified, and to appreciate his adopted country all the better afterwards, Michel occasionally spends his holidays in his other homeland, the United States. There he takes advantage of the opportunity to check up on the Californian vineyards that worry the French so. The article he wrote on his return from one of his latest visits didn't cram the reader full of facts and statistics on fermentation temperatures, selected yeasts or the quality of American oaks. It was about the almost arrogant beauty of the region. A paradise on earth, with cool morning mists, hot Provençal afternoons, and an air heavy with the scent of wild oleanders. He concluded that in this garden of Eden a refined civilisation is beginning to emerge: 'Their vegetables are superb, they even make goat's cheese!'

And over there, as well as in France, wine men bring together culture, feeling and taste.

CONCLUSION

FIERCELY INDEPENDENT, slightly anarchistic, the characters in this book do not easily give in. But are they a dying breed?

Eloi Dürrbach's priority is to buy the best winery equipment available before he thinks about installing central heating for his family. At the same time he plants vines that risk destroying his right to the appellation. Bruno Clair dynamites soils thought to be unfarmable and reduces his vines' yields to the lowest limit bearable. Nicolas Joly left the world of Eurodollars for La Coulée de Serrant and a chemical-free agriculture. Léonard Humbrecht complicates an already confusing domaine by introducing a Burgundian vine variety into Alsace.

French vineyards today still produce some wonderful surprises, off the beaten track of fashionable neat, clean and tedious wines made for consumers in search of superficial sensations.

Burgundy has woken up, Bordeaux often reaches perfection, the Loire is being rediscovered, and Alsace is next in line. Even the south gets round to creating a few masterpieces.

But it would be wrong if these *terroirs* and vintages, watched over by a few faithful shepherds, were to become museum pieces. More materialist shadows loom on the horizon. New vineyard owners have appeared filling the role once occupied by the Church: multinationals, banks, insurance companies, and conglomerates of all kinds are taking over family domaines that are up for sale because of the ill-adapted French inheritance laws and the insane increase in the price of prime vineyard land.

Such sociological changes are bound to have repercussions on the type of wine produced. Will these large modern companies know how to find and keep exceptional characters such as Claude Ricard at the Domaine de Chevalier, or Jean-Paul Hardère at Latour, who devote their whole lives to their wines? Or will these companies, influenced by the culture surrounding them, prefer to employ competent technicians, paid to avoid taking risks, who will make wines that may be perfect technically but are indistinguishable from those of their neighbours?

ADDRESSES

The following includes addresses of winemakers mentioned in the book, as well as others whose wines I particularly enjoy.

ALSACE

Marcel Deiss et Fils, 15 route du Vin, 68750 Bergheim
tel: 89.73.63.37
Works hard at making a real Alsace red wine rather than a rosé called red. Also makes succulent whites.

Mme Colette Faller, Clos des Capucins, Kientzheim, 68240 Kaysersberg
tel: 89.47.13.21
When she first married, Colette Faller knew nothing about wine. After her husband's death she took over the domaine and produces world-famous wines.

André Kientzler, 50 Route de Bergheim, 68150 Ribeauvillé
tel:89.73.67.10
Has a handful of *Grands Crus*, plenty of common sense and a few crazy ideas such as harvesting in December to produce ice wines.

ADDRESSES

André Ostertag, 87 rue Finkwiller, 67680 Epfig
tel: 88.85.51.34.
André studied oenology in Burgundy. This explains why he's
fascinated by the influence on his family's wines of ageing in oak
and of the differences in *terroirs*.

BEAUJOLAIS

Lucien Charmet, Le Bois D'oingt, 69620 Le Breuil
tel: 74.71.64.83
Beaujolais as it tasted before M. Chaptal thought of chaptalisation!
Light and delicious.

BORDEAUX

Margaux

Jean-Luc Vonderheyden, Ch. Monbrison, Arsac, 33460 Margaux
tel: 56.58.84.36
An ex-photographer who took over his mother's domaine and has
become more of a perfectionist than many of his colleagues. At a
recent meeting on improving the quality of *Crus Bourgeois*, he
suggested that maximum permitted yields be further restricted.
Few agreed because smaller yields mean fewer bottles to sell. That
night some of his vines were savagely pruned – an unsigned
warning not to raise the subject again.

Ch. Labégorce-Zédé, Soussans, 33460 Margaux
tel: 56.88.71.31
Those who were brought up thinking that Margaux are feminine
wines should try this version: muscular, robust and seductive.

Moulis

Ch. Poujeaux, Moulis, 33480 Castelnau-de-Médoc
tel: 56.58.02.96
A classic.

St-Julien

Ch. Léoville-Las-Cases, Saint-Julien-Beychevelle, 33250 Pauillac
tel: 56.69.25.26
A second growth edging its way towards the quality of first growths.

Graves

Ch. Carmes Haut-Brion, 197 Ave Jean Cordier 33600 Pessac
tel: 56.51.49.43/56.48.28.12
A doll's-house vineyard surrounded by Bordeaux's suburbs. The owner's son-in-law gave up his career to concentrate on producing a great wine. Good value ... for the time being.

Ch. Respide-Médeville, Preignac, 33210 Langon
tel: 56.63.27.59
Excellent red and white Graves made by M. Médeville. He also owns the famous Château Gilette, a Sauternes aged at the Château for at least twenty years before it is released.

Sauternes/Barsac

Robert Lamothe, Ch. Haut-Bergeron, 33210 Preignac
tel: 56.63.24.76
Little known, first-rate.

Fronsac

Paul Barre, Ch. La Grave, 33126 Fronsac
tel: 57.51.64.95

Another producer seriously considering going over to biodynamic farming. But even now his wines already have tremendous depth and concentration.

St-Emilion

Mme. Danièle André, Ch. Haut-Segottes, 33330 St-Emilion
tel: 57.24.60.98
Mme. André tends the vineyards with the same care as a rose garden. Her winery is as tidy as her kitchen. Her wine combines ripe plummy fruit and elegance but avoids the vulgar jammy taste that some other Saint-Emilion *Grand Crus* have acquired.

BURGUNDY

Jacques Seysses, Domaine Dujac, 7 rue de la Bussière, Morey-St-Denis, 21220 Gevrey-Chambertin
tel: 80.34.32.58
Jacques Seysses is an open-minded newcomer to the wine world. He bought his property in 1968 and has recently acquired the Domaine La Triennes in Provence.

Georges Chicotot, 9 rue Paul Cabet, 21700 Nuit-Saint-Georges.
tel: 80.61.19.33
Deep, voluptuous Nuits-Saint-Georges made by an impassioned producer.

Leroy, Auxey-Duresses, 21190 Meursault
tel: 80.21.21.10
The world-famous maison Leroy is part owner of the Romanée-Conti.

Hubert de Montille, Volnay, 21190 Meursault
tel:80.41.71. 79/80.21.62.67
Volnay and Pommard made to perfection.

Guffens-Heynen, Pouilly-Fuissé, Vergisson, 71960 Pierreclos
tel: 85.35.84.22
Its Belgian owner insists on minute yields.

Michel Juillot, BP 10 Mercurey, 71640 Givry
tel: 85.45.27.27
The whole family, parents and children, happily make and promote
luscious wines from their home town.

CHAMPAGNE

Pierre Barbier-Beaufort, 51150 Trépail
tel: 26.50.12.34
A great champagne aged in oak by a small producer – who comes
from Alsace!

Bollinger, 4 Bd du Maréchal de Lattre de Tassigny, BP 4, 51160
Ay
tel:26.55.21.31
'The' quality champagne house.

CÔTES DU RHÔNE (NORTH)

Côte Rôtie

Marcel Guigal, 69420 Ampuis, Condrieu
tel: 74.56.10.22
The king of the Côtes Rôties.

Hermitage

Gérard Chave, Mauves, 07300 Tournon-sur-Rhône
tel: 75.08.24.63
Don't bother going to his domaine. There's never anything for
sale. But it's well worth keeping an eye out in restaurants or in
wine shops for his exceptional red and white Hermitage.

Saint-Joseph

J-L. Grippat, La Sauva, 07300 Tournon-sur-Rhône
tel: 75.08.15.51
A man of tradition producing a deep, violet-scented Saint-Joseph –
a winter delight for those who like tannic, fleshy, sensuous
reds.

CÔTES DU RHÔNE (SOUTH)

J-P Cartier, Domaine Les Goubert, Gigondas, 84190 Beaumes-de-Venise
tel: 90.65.86.38
Makes a wonderfully plummy Gigondas and an aromatic
red Beaumes-de-Venise. Is another great believer in unfiltered
wines.

*M. Steinmaier, Domaine Ste-Anne, Mas Les Celettes, St-Gervais,
30200 Bagnols-sur-Mer*
tel: 66.82.77.41
Apart from his excellent generic Côtes du Rhône, this ex-
Burgundian winemaker produces a very small quantity of white
from the Viognier grape. Until recently, this grape was only planted
in Condrieu where it produces the famous Château Grillet. Steinmaier's Viognier is a discrete, less perfumed version. Its big
advantage is that it can be drunk with food. Goes best with
scrambled eggs and truffles.

Châteauneuf-du-Pape

M. Reynaud, Ch. Rayas, 84230 Châteauneuf-du-Pape
tel: 90.83.73.09
M. Reynaud is easily the most eccentric character of Châteauneuf-
du Pape. According to Eloi Dürrbach at the Domaine de Trévallon,
the best wine in the world is a Rayas 1945.

Ch. de Beaucastel, 84350 Courthézon
tel: 90.70.70.60
This is one of the rare Châteauneuf-du-Pape domaines that has planted all thirteen permitted vine varieties. The chemical-free vineyard covers a vast area of seventy hectares and produces a top-quality red and white.

LANGUEDOC

Gilbert Alquier et Fils, Faugères, 34600 Bedarieux
tel: 67.23.07.89
A wonderfully fragrant, spicy, southern wine.

LOIRE
Muscadet de Sèvre-et-Maine

M. Boullault et fils, Domaine des Dorices, 44330 Vallet
tel: 40.33.95.30
The Boullaults produce a Muscadet that is real wine and not a thirst-quencher. It has flavour and is one of the few in the region made to be kept for at least six years.

Guy Bossard, La Bretonnière, 44430 Le Landreau
tel: 40.06.40.91 fax: 40.06.46.79
With this wine there is no risk of the splitting headache that some Muscadets cause. M. Bossard produces a delicious crisp, dry 'organic' Muscadet.

Anjou Rouge

Didier Richou, Domaine Richou, Chauvigné, Mozé-sur-Louet, 49190
Rochefort-sur-Loire
tel: 41.78.72.13
Two good value reds made here by the young and enthusiastic Didier. The light, fruity Gamay provides more pleasure than most Beaujolais. His Cabernet Franc produced from old vines should really be kept a few years. But it also tastes good young.

Coteaux du Layons

This appellation produces sweet wines from the Chenin grape, similar in style to Sauternes but with a crisp lemon acidity. The actor Gérard Depardieu and the famous French cook Lenotre have recently bought châteaux here. It won't be long before Coteaux du Layons become fashionable and expensive.

M. Boivin, Ch. de Fesles, 49380 Thouarcé
tel: 41.54.14.32
This is the domaine that has just been bought by Lenotre. Needless to say he chose one of the best. It will be interesting to see if the gentle and somewhat retiring M. Boivin will continue to make 'his' own wine as he has always done without interference.

M. Lalanne, Ch. de Bellerive, 49190 Rochefort-sur-Loire
tel: 41.78.33.66
This producer owns most of the minute appellation Quarts de Chaume. His semi-sweet and sweet wines take about fifteen years to open out. But the wait is well worthwhile.

Saumur-Champigny

A classic example of how an appellation can destroy itself. In the case of Saumur-Champigny its great wines long went unnoticed. Now the region has become trendy and the wines are in great demand. Producers have increased their yields and in many cases the quality has dropped.

Ch. de Chaintres, 49460 Dampierre-sur-Loire
tel: 41.52.90.54
One of the first producers to have worked hard at promoting the wines from this appellation when they were unknown. The wines are still delicious and have character.

Les frères Foucault, 62 Place Collier, 49400 Chacé
tel: 41.52.94.66
Another style of Champigny – unique in its own way. The three
Foucault brothers produce a delicious organic wine aged in one-
year-old casks bought from various great domaines. Burgundy fans
can taste a Champigny with a Romanée-Conti flavour; Bordeaux
lovers can try the Margaux-tainted Saumur.

White Saumur

Roger Vachet-Bremard, rue des Déportés, Turquant, 49730 Mont-
soreau
tel: 41.38.11.21
An old-style white Saumur: mouth-watering fresh with a dry
chalky flavour.

Saint-Nicolas-de-Bourgueil

Joël Taluau, Domaine de la Chevrette, St-Nicolas-de-Bourgueil,
37140 Bourgueil
tel: 47.97.78.79
Taluau doesn't believe in oak. His *Vielles Vignes* aged in stainless
steel should shake up those who only believe in traditional methods.

Chinon

Bernard Baudry, Coteau de Sonnay, Cravant-les-Coteaux, 37500
Chinon
tel: 47.93.15.79
Bernard produces a ready-to-drink Chinon for the impatient, and
a more tannic one, partly aged in oak casks, for connoisseurs.

Philippe Alliet, L'Ouche-Monde, Cravant-les-Coteaux, 37500
Chinon
tel: 47.93.17.62
A perfectionist, nicknamed the 'Bordelais' of Chinon because his
wines are so firm, severe and elegant.

Montlouis et Vouvray

These two appellations are often forgotten, despite the extra-ordinary range of white wines they produce: dry, *demi-sec*, sweet, *méthode champenoise*, *pétillant*. The top producers make sparkling wines that are better than many champagnes, and semi-sweet wines that can be drunk with fish as well as poultry. As for sweet wines, there is no rival to the luscious 1989 and 1990 vintages which will happily keep for over one hundred years.

Claude Levasseur, 38 rue des Bouvineries, Husseau, 37270 Montlouis-sur-Loire
tel: 47.50.84.53
Worth a visit just to hear M. Levasseur speak with the purest of French accents and to taste the most subtle Montlouis.

Philippe Foreau, Le Clos Naudin, 37210 Vouvray
tel: 47.52.71.87
Philippe is a serious gambler when it comes to bringing in his grapes: if the late autumn weather is sunny, he wins and harvests ultra-ripe grapes producing some of the richest, most honeyed wines of the appellation; if it rains, he loses.

M. Huet, Domaine du Haut Lieu, 37210 Vouvray
tel: 47.52.78.87
For a number of years, M. Pinguet the owner's son-in-law, tried out biodynamic farming on part of the domaine. He's now per-suaded that it produces a better quality grape, and so the whole vineyard is being turned over to it. His wines, along with Foreau's, are without doubt the best of the appellation.

Pouilly Fumé

Across the river Loire from Sancerre, this appellation produces whites also from the Sauvignon grape. It's easier to find a decent

Pouilly-Fumé even though the Sancerre vineyard is three times as large.

Didier Dagueneau, St-Andelain, 58150 Pouilly-sur-Loire
tel: 86.39.15.62
The most expensive producer of the appellation. But that doesn't stop his Cuvée Silex – produced from very old vines planted on flinty soils and aged in oak – from being snapped up by connoisseurs.

ROUSSILLON

Banyuls

Les frères Parcé, 54 Avenue du Puig-del-Mas, 66650 Banyuls-sur-Mer
tel: 68.88.32.93
Banyuls is the French equivalent to port and it's just about the only French wine that can stand up to chocolate. Worth drinking at least once with sardines, as the locals do!

SAVOIE

Michel Grisard, Fréterive, 73250 St-Pierre d'Albigny
tel: 79.28.62.10
When skiing nearby, branch out from the unexciting Gamay de Savoie 'pour les touristes' and try the Mondeuse, the classic Savoie variety similar to the Syrah grape. Grisard's is aromatic, tannic and velvety.

Madiran

Vigneau-Tachoueres, Ch. Pichard, Soublecause, 65700 Maubourguet
tel: 62.96.35.73
On the whole Madirans have undergone the same fate as Cahors.
They've lost their identity, taste like an uninteresting Bordeaux
and are sold at twice the price. This Madiran has real personality.
Delicious and still good value.

GLOSSARY

Appellation: A clearly defined topological area. The *appellation contrôlée* label acts as a certificate guaranteeing the wine's place of origin and the standards associated with that area

Blanc de blancs: A sparkling white wine or champagne made exclusively from white grapes instead of the traditional champagne method using a blend of black and white grapes

Bombage: The submergence of grape skins in grape juice to extract maximum colour and aroma – also known as *pigeage*

Botrytis Cinerea: a mushroom that attacks grapes. Depending on the climatic conditions it can either cause grey rot – detrimental to a harvest – or noble rot producing some of the finest sweet white wines

Cap: This is the thick, hard, compact layer formed by the solid parts of the grapes (pips, skins, stalks) in a fermentation vat. The carbon dioxide released during the fermentation forces these solid parts to float on top of the juice

Chaptalisation: The adding of sugar to wine during fermentation to increase the wine's alcohol content (hence, non-chaptalised wines)

Climat: Term used in Burgundy to refer to a specific vineyard site or *lieux-dit*

Clonal-selected vines: Identical vines produced from a gene pool to guarantee disease-free crops and give preordained characteristics

Clos: Originally, a walled vineyard or vineyard once enclosed by a wall. These occur mainly in Burgundy. Specific vineyards which are sufficiently distinguished gain the privilege of being singled out as a 'clos'

Cubitainer: A plastic container, holding five to twenty litres of wine, used for selling wine in bulk for everyday drinking

Cuvée: literally means the contents of a vat (*cuvé*), but can mean the wine bottled from a vat, or the wine bottled from a specific blend

Jeunes Vignes: Young vines

Lees: Sediment that falls to the bottom of a vat during or after fermentation

Lieux-dits: a specific vineyard site usually named after a historic or geographic feature

Machine à piger: A machine that crushes and treads red grapes. It enables the juice to remain in contact with the grape skins and stalks and so extract colour and tannin from them

Malolactic fermentation: Also known as secondary fermentation. Involves the transformation of harsher malic acid (the one found in green apples) into gentler lactic acid (the one found in milk), producing softer wines.

Métayage: share-cropping. A system often used in Burgundy whereby the wine grower pays rent by handing over part of his harvest

Négociant: Wine wholesaler/shipper who buys grapes or wine in bulk, blends and bottles

Noble rot: Under the right climatic conditions the *Botrytis Cinerea* fungus attacks white grapes concentrating the sugar content. It gives sweet white wines with characteristic aromas of honey and candied orange peel

Non-dosé: An ultra-dry champagne or white wine to which no sugar is added before corking and dispatching

Oak-ageing: The ageing of red and white wine in new oak casks

Pigeage: Occurs during the fermentation of red wines. The process consists of submerging and macerating the cap (grape skins, pips, stalks) in the grape juice in order to extract colour and tannin

Pigeou: A long stick with a flat disk at one end used to break up and submerge the cap during the fermentation of red wines

Racking: The siphoning-off of wine from its lees by pumping the clear wine into a clean cask or vat

Sélection de Grains Nobles: Appears on labels of exceptionally sweet wines when they have been made from late-picked, individually selected grapes. A term essentially used for Alsace wines

Terroir: The particular nature of a soil that gives its flavour to wine produced from it

Vendange: Grape harvest

Vendanges Tardives: Literally late harvested grapes, producing sweet wines. A term essentially used for Alsace wines

Vieilles vignes: Old vines

Vin de garde: A wine which requires bottle-age – around a minimum of ten years – to reach full maturity (hence, *bouteille de garde*)

Vin jaune: Jura sherry-like speciality made of late-picked Savagin grapes aged in barrel for at least six years

INDEX

Subjects such as 'Château Latour' are indexed as 'Latour, Château'

Accad, Guy 132
Allied Lyons 81
Aloxe-Corton-les-Maréchaudes 117
Alsace 135–43, 148, 155
Amboise 7

Bailey, Jenny 89–96
Banyuls 108–9
Beaujolais 8, 10, 102
Beaune 117
Benais 27
Bernard, Olivier 68, 71
Besse, Jean-Baptiste 105–13
Bettane, Michel 35, 36, 40, 55, 145–53
biodynamic farming 49–52, 55
Bize-Leroy, Madame 55
Bollinger 151
bombage (*pigeage*) 15, 20–21, 74, 94, 130–1
Bordeaux 8–9, 19, 63, 64, 65, 67–75, 77–87, 90–96, 110, 155
Botrytis cinerea ('noble rot') 53, 54, 139
Bourgogne Aligoté 118
Bourgueil 27–34, 35–6
Bourgueil, Abbaye de 18
Borgeuil, St Nicolas de 36–43
Bucher winepress 26
Burgundy 14, 27, 58, 63, 64, 93, 115–25, 127–33, 150, 155

Cabernet Franc 18, 19, 31, 35, 95

Cabernet Sauvignon 18, 95, 99, 100
Calon-Ségur 152
'cap' 21, 31
Chalon, Château 45
Chambertin 117
Chambertin-Clos de Bèze 118, 124
Chambertin-Musigny 152
Chambolle-Musigny 117, 122, 129, 152
chaptalisation 8, 15, 53
Chardonnay 5, 116, 118, 122, 143
Châteauneuf-du-Pape 100
Chave, Gérard 103
Chêne Vert 18–20
Chenin 31, 47, 55
Chevalier, Domaine de 63, 68–75, 156
Chinon 7, 15, 18–20, 31, 35
Clair, Bruno 115–25, 155
Clair, Joseph 118–19, 123
Clair, Michel 122
Clair-Daü, Domaine 123
Clair-Daü rosé 119
climate 83–4
climats 117, 119–20
clonal selection 40, 55, 100
Clos des Capucins 156
Clos de la Dioterie 14, 15–16
Clos Saint-Urbain 138–43
Clos Vougeot 127, 128, 131–2
Clos Windsbuhl 143
Condrieu 104

Confuron, Bernadette 128, 129, 130, 131, 132
Confuron, Jacky 127–33
conical vats 29, 31
Corton-Bressandes 117
Corton-Charlemagne 150
Cos d'Estournel, Château 110
Côte de Nuits 127–33
Côte-Rotie 152
Coteaux du Layon 31, 48
Côtes du Brulhois 59, 66
Côtes-du-Rhône 152
Côtes du Ventoux 11
Coulée de Serrant 45–55, 155
Couve de Murville, Jacques 82
Cowdray, Lord, 82
Curnonsky (food critic) 45
Cussac 77, 78
Cuvée des Petits Pères 11

Dijon 118, 119
Dion, Roger 35n, 83n
Dobson, Charles 91, 96
Druet, Martine 27, 28, 29
Druet, Pierre-Jacques 25–34
Dujac, Domaine 93
Dürrbach, Eloi 97–104, 155
Dürrbach, Floriane 102

Echézeaux 128, 131

Faller, Colette 156
fining 54
Forts de Latour, Les 83, 86

Gamay 118
Gardère, Jean-Paul 77–87, 156
Gevrey-Chambertin 117, 118, 124
Gewürztraminer 135, 136, 138
Giscard d'Estaing, Valéry 82
Grand Mont 28, 32
Graves 67–75

Grillet, Château 45
Giugal, Marcel 152
Guigné, Count Charles de 90, 91, 95
Guyot, Dr 99

Hanson, Anthony 127
Haut-Brion 67, 69, 78, 147
Heath, Edward 82
Henocq, Philibert 60–61
Hoffman, Dustin 64
Humbrecht, Ginette 138, 142
Humbrecht, Léonard 135–43, 148, 152, 155
Humbrecht, Olivier 139

Institut National des Appellations d'Origine (INAO) 99, 104, 143

jeunes vignes 17
Joguet, Charles 13–23
Joly, Nicolas 45–56, 155

Kientzler, André 152

La Mouline 152
La Taille 36–43
Lafite 151
Lafite-Rothschild 78
Lafon, Count René 147
Lagraulière 110
Latour, Château 64, 77–87, 151, 156
Latour, Louis 137
Legay, Guy 63
Legrand, Francine 12
Legrand, Lucie 3, 12
Legrand, Lucien 1–12, 42
Legrand, Yves 12
Léoville-Las Cases, Château 63, 152
Lepré, Georges 57–66

Leroy, Domaine 55
Les Languettes 150
Les Longeroies 119
Les Varennes 17
Les Vaudenelles 119
Loire Valley 14–22, 27–34, 35–43, 45–55, 155
Louis XIV 46
Louis XV 90

Mabileau, Jules 35–44
Magnan, Edmond 32–3
malolactic fermentation 40, 100
Margaux 67, 78, 80, 152
Marsannay 118–21, 123–5
Martin, Henri 82
Médoc 67, 77, 80–86, 90–96, 109, 137
Merlot 95
Meursault 117, 146, 147
Montaigne, Michel de 138
Montlouis 31
Montrachet 45
Morey-Saint-Denis 93, 121–2
Moulis 158
Mouton 78, 151
Muscat 136, 152

National Institute of Agricultural Research (INRA) 22, 40
'noble rot' 53, 54, 139
Nuits-Saint-Georges 117, 127, 129

oak-ageing 11n, 32
Oliver, Raymond 60, 61, 62

Paris:
    Le Grand Véfour 60–61, 62
    Ritz 57, 58–9, 62–6
    Rue de la Banque (No. 1) 1–12
    Rue de la Montane-Sainte-Geneviève (No. 48) 105–13

Parker, Robert 97
Pauillac 67
Pearson group 81, 82, 85, 86
Petit Verdot 95
Pétrus 64
Peynaud, Professor 71, 72
phylloxera 22
Pichard, Château 167
pigeage (bombage) 15, 20–21, 74, 94, 130–1
Pinguet, M. 164
Pinot Blanc 136, 137
Pinot Gris 143
Piot Gris/Tokay 136
Pinot Noir 5, 116, 118, 119, 121, 122, 127, 132, 136
Pollock, Lord 82
Provence 97–104
Puisais, Jacques 14, 16, 18, 21, 28

Quié, Paul 80
Quinto do Noval Nacional 64

Rabelais, François 35
racking 16
Rahoul, Château 91
Rauzan-Gassies, Château 80
Rayas, Château 100
Ricard, Claude 67–75, 156
Richou, Didier 161
Riesling 135, 136, 137, 139
Ritz, César 66
Roche-aux-Moines 47, 54
Romanée-Conti 127

Saint-Emilion 27, 67, 109
Saint-Julien 67
Saint-Nicolas-de-Bourgueil 36–43
Saint-Simon, Duc de 9n
Saumur-Champigny 27, 31
Sauvignon 47, 71, 72, 95, 99
Savennières 30, 31

Savigny-les-Beaune-la-
    Dominode 124
Sélections de Grains Nobles 139, 140
Sémillon 71, 95
Sénéjac, Château 90–96
Seysses, Jacques 93
soils 19, 32, 38, 39, 49, 53, 54, 67,
    78, 83, 94, 98, 99, 101, 120, 121,
    124, 137, 139, 143
Soltner, André 141
Souillac 60
Steiner, Rudolf 49
Sylvaner 136, 137
Syrah 99, 100

Taffonneau, M. 15
Tahon, M. 75
terroir 42, 83, 86, 101, 135, 136–7,
    139, 141, 143, 150

Thann 138
Thunn, Mrs 51
Thustrup, Peter 57, 58
Tokay 139, 141
Touraine 15, 35
Trévallon, Domaine de 97–104
typicité 49, 53

Vendanges Tardives 139, 140
vieilles vins 18
Vignelaure, Château 100, 102
Viognier 104
Vogüé, Domaine de 147
Vonderheyden, Jean-Luc 91
Vosne-Romanée 116, 117, 127–33
Vouvray 31, 48

Yquem, Château 45, 53, 64